To Russell and Bob
from

Mother & Dad

Dec. 25, 1957

D1482699

My Friends, the Huskies

My Friends, the Huskies

BY RICHARD DOVERS

Farrar, Straus and Cudahy · New York

MANUFACTURED IN THE UNITED STATES OF AMERICA

AMERICAN BOOK—STRATFORD PRESS, INC., NEW YORK

FOREWORD

by SIR DOUGLAS MAWSON
O.B.E., F.R.S., D.SC., B.E.

This book supplies eloquent testimony that the author is of a type born to face and endure the trials and hazards of polar exploration. His father, George Dovers, before him also proved his ability as an Antarctic explorer, for it was he who in 1912 surveyed that part of the coast of Queen Mary Land where the Russian Geophysical Year expedition is now based.

Robert is true to type and, though professionally a cartographer, has proved himself a master of sledge travel either by dog team or by tractor. He emerged from the last war with a good combatant record in New Guinea and elsewhere, in time to join in the post-war upsurge of Australian activity in the Far South. He was one of the first-year party to occupy Heard Island in what has become known as the Australian National Antarctic Research Expedition. As a result mainly of Dovers's field activities on that desolate and mountainous sub-Antarctic terrain, the Expedition has published an excellent map of Heard Island with details of its glaciers and volcanic features.

Robert Dovers continued until recently as a member of the staff of A.N.A.R.E. He was entrusted with the leadership of the first party to occupy the important Antarctic Base, Mawson, established on the coast of MacRobertson Land. There, by dog sledge and weasel transport he, with the help of his companions, completed much of the detailed charting of 250 miles of coastline and penetrated the ice-cap of the hinterland for a distance of 150 miles from the sea. That was in 1954–5.

However, the present story is of his adventures in Terre Adélie as an interlude in his A.N.A.R.E. activities. There by the good offices of Phillip Law, Director of the Antarctic Division of the Commonwealth Department of External Affairs, he was attached, during their 1952 operations, to the French expedition organized by M. Paul-Émile Victor. At the invitation of the French, he was to learn all he could of Polar exploration from experienced French personnel, at the same time benefiting all by his competency in other fields.

The official reports of the French expedition are to be found in the voluminous publications of that undertaking. Dovers's story is an account, in intimate detail, of his own experiences. As he had so much to do with the dog teams, he has concentrated on the behaviour and psychology of the sledge dogs. Hence the title of the book: *My Friends, the Huskies.*

So fully and ably are the ways and lives of the dogs pictured herein, that this book is not only a story of adventure but will remain a valuable record of the habits and temperament of these animals. It will be observed that in some ways these huskies are, as yet, little differentiated from their Arctic wolf ancestors; but are firmly linked with man for mutual benefit.

AUTHOR'S NOTE

The reader will perhaps find it curious as he reads this book that nowhere is any reference made to my experiencing any difficulties from being one lone Australian amid a group of Frenchmen. This is because at all times I was treated as one of the party and now in writing I remain in that same frame of mind that I had with them; there was no question of nationality, I remained always one of them.

This happy state of affairs was due to no virtue of mine but was derived purely from their kindness and politeness, which I can only presume to be a national characteristic. For a very brief period on the ship, perhaps, I felt otherwise than one of them in my role of observer. Christmas at sea dispelled this. On Christmas day it was customary with them for the leader of the party to hand out presents entrusted to him by friends and relatives of the men. I stood by whilst this was being done and thought it a nice custom. To my surprise, Garcia pushed a large parcel into my hands. I thanked him and expressed my surprise and gratitude at this small act of thoughtfulness. It was Garcia's turn to be surprised.

'But,' he said, 'you are one of us.'

When I examined the parcel I noticed that Garcia's name had been erased and my own substituted.

Thus I became one of them, and so remained throughout the year.

There is no formal expression of obligation to Paul-Émile Victor and his men in this book. I trust that the whole book expresses my gratitude and obligation to him and them for the privilege of serving with them and sharing their adventures.

R. G. DOVERS

Contents

1
———————

A Change of Plan

The Norwegian sealer *Tottan* was standing against the
edge of the sea ice that was still barring the way into Port
Martin, the French base in Terre Adélie, Antarctica. For
two weeks the ship had been steaming along the edge of the
ice waiting for it to break out, as it always does each year,
and let her inshore to Port Martin to carry out the relief of
the party of French scientists who had passed the year there.
On board were a party of twelve scientists and technicians,
who were to take over from the existing party and maintain
their work for another year in this, the windiest corner of the
world. So far the only contact with those on shore was by
radio, but this day most of us were scanning the miles of
featureless frozen sea for a party that was to come off from
the shore with a dog team to establish contact, and collect
their year-old mail.

At the ship's side were a group of Adelie penguins, funny,
inquisitive little folk that are found all along the thousands of
miles of Antarctica's coastline. No one ever tires of watching
penguins, and, in turn, Adelie penguins never seem to tire of
watching men. These are the universal penguin of the Antarctic. Whenever explorers have touched on the pack ice or on
the shore in these far southern waters, they have found
groups of these little black and white people waiting on the
water's edge to welcome them, and the moment a man sets
his foot ashore a group of Adelie penguins comes fussing up

to inspect him. A sailor was ashore on the floe, teasing a group of them, for everybody in the Antarctic finds them irresistible. The penguins regarded the man with a mixture of curiosity and distrust; the more prudent keeping a safe distance away, while the less fearful kept advancing closer and closer. From time to time the man caught one and there was a great flapping of flippers and pecks of beaks, while the friends of the victim advanced on the man uttering sharp little cries with the ruffs of their neck feathers blown out with anger. Considering the relative sizes, for an Adelie penguin only stands fourteen inches high, they are most courageous little animals. Even when released, none the worse for his experience except for his outraged dignity, the victim did not take to flight but retreated a few paces and turned and faced his aggressor. He seemed much less afraid than angry with what he considered, no doubt, a show of particularly bad manners.

However, interest was soon lost in the man and the penguins when someone saw a few black dots on the sea ice between the ship and the shore. A quick check with binoculars identified these dots as a dog team and a sledge on its way to the ship. Of all on board I was naturally the most interested in the dogs for they were to be my charges in the coming year. The others were much more interested in the men coming off to the ship from the station, for the men with the team were friends of some on board and all were interested to know how they had found their year in Adélie Land.

In a very short time the sledge was at the ship, a steel pin was driven into the ice to moor the sledge and the two bearded men in travel-stained windproofs were clambering aboard. The dogs made a quick inspection of the sledge and in usual husky fashion showed their opinion of it and its cargo by lifting their legs against it. This done they flopped down on the ice and with tongues hanging out looked about

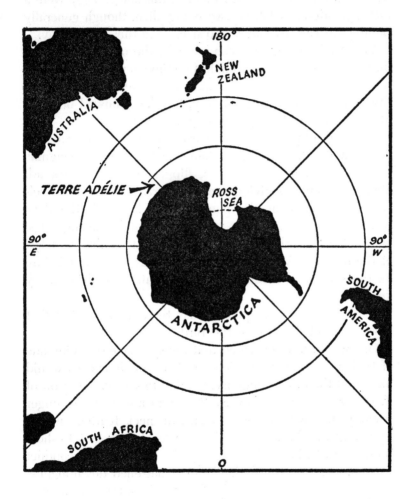

in lazy interest at what was going on. I cannot say that I was greatly impressed with them at this stage. They were a rather nondescript lot, no two being alike, though generally big dogs of various shapes and sizes. And they were filthy.

The Adelie penguins, who were on the other side of the ship when the sledge arrived, lost no time in waddling around to inspect the new arrivals. Apart from slightly pricking up their ears and watching intently, the dogs showed no signs of excitement as the penguins approached.

The leading penguin was a yard from one of the crouched dogs when it happened! He had wandered up as penguins do, head cocked on one side, flippers slightly outspread, obviously bent on giving the new arrivals a friendly welcome. The moment the penguin was in reach the dogs sprang, there was a mass of snapping and snarling dogs, one or two pitiful strangled squawks and all that was left of the little black and white creature was an ugly red stain on the snow and a few bedraggled feathers drifting away down-wind.

It all happened so quickly that there was nothing that anyone could do to save the bird.

One would have expected that the spectacle of seeing one of their number torn to pieces in front of their eyes would have sent the other penguins scuttling to safety. Not a bit of it. On the contrary, they continued to advance, no longer friendly, but with flippers outspread, neck feathers fluffed up in anger and uttering shrill squawks of rage, as if to show these uncouth barbarians of dogs that their sort of conduct was not at all appreciated. The dogs flattened down against the snow and waited. Only the timely intervention of a sailor, who took the penguins one by one by the scruff of their necks and threw them still vigorously protesting into the nearby water, saved them from a massacre.

Meanwhile on board there was much handshaking. The two bearded men who had climbed on board proved to be

Michel Barré, leader of the party ashore, and Georges Schwartz, who had been looking after the dogs for the past year.

Jackie Duhamel, one of our relieving members, who had been here the year previously, was down at the team patting a large Labrador type of dog, the general appearance of which made all the rest look well groomed by comparison.

'This is Aspirin, isn't it?' he called out to Barré who was leaning over the rail. The reply was affirmative. This did not convey a great deal to me at the time; apart from his extra low standard of cleanliness the dog did not seem to be a particularly interesting one, but it was not very long before I got to know Aspirin quite well.

'We bought one team of dogs from the English,' explained Mario Marret; 'that is, we bought seven dogs and they threw in Aspirin for luck saying, "He's not much good, in fact no good at all, but you will find him amusing!" '

By the time the sledge and team were ready to leave again, loaded down with mail and fresh fruit for those still on shore, I had had time to examine the team and make their acquaintance. This was a team of the older dogs known as 'Pickles' team' after Pickles, the big leader. They were all in fine condition, which was particularly impressive as they had only returned two days ago from a 300-mile journey on the Polar plateau. But save for Aspirin they were still just so many dogs for me. A little later they were speeding on their way shorewards in a rather erratic course, deviating from the home route from time to time as they sighted successive groups of penguins, for on the sea ice in summer a journey frequently degenerates into a gambol from one group of penguins to another despite a considerable amount of blasphemy from the driver.

I should have liked to have kept the doings of men completely out of this story and written only of the dogs, but the lives of the men and of the dogs were so mingled in their years together that it becomes necessary to tell the story of the men as well to provide the background for the doings and ways of the dogs.

I was a member of the staff of the Antarctic Division, Department of External Affairs of Australia, posted as Australian observer with the Third French Antarctic Expedition and destined to spend a year with that group in their station on Terre Adélie, Antarctica, at their base at Port Martin. This base had already been manned for two years by successive parties and our group of nine men under René Garcia were to take over the station for the third year. It was planned to place a group of three men, under Mario Marret, some fifty miles west at Pointe Géologie, to study for a year the life of the Emperor penguin; for at Pointe Géologie had been found the fourth known rookery in the world of these primitive and curious birds.

After a further week of waiting, the ice barring the way finally broke out and the *Tottan* was able to penetrate to Port Martin and tie up alongside a convenient cliff a short distance from the station. The interim had been used to good advantage as far as I and the dogs were concerned, for during that period we were able to kill and skin twenty seals while cruising among the pack ice, and that seal meat meant many months of food for the dogs for the coming year. One advantage of life in the Antarctic is that because of the low temperature all this meat could just be dumped on the snow and left until required without fear of it going bad.

The ship was only tied up for two days at Port Martin, in which time all stores were unloaded, and the majority of the new party, including myself, were put ashore. This done the ship sailed for Pointe Géologie to put ashore Marret and his little group and their stores and equipment. With it sailed a number of the old and new Port Martin parties to aid in the work of unloading the Point Géologie team.

As soon as I was ashore Georges Schwartz introduced me to all the dogs. The first I met were Bjorn's team, comprising mainly three-year-olds, a fine team of dogs at their best age for work. At this stage this team consisted of Bjorn, the leader, a great, powerful but not over-intelligent dog; Fram, his lieutenant, a heavy stocky dog rather like an Alsatian; Milk and Tiki, the two inseparables, and the two bitches, Helen and Ifaut. Ifaut proved to be a beautiful intelligent and gentle animal while Helen, a small black animal resembling an Australian kelpie, seemed quite out of place among the other five typical sledge dogs. I was rather shocked at the time to find this poor little dog included in a dog team when she seemed more suited to a life as a pet in a surburban home. I did not realize then, as I was later to discover, that under that veneer of a small black kelpie was almost pure wolf and a mass of muscle and sinew that was tireless, even when the others were nearly dropping from fatigue. And she had a degree of savageness that could be startling, even when one knew her well!

At the other side of the hut was the second dog line, Boss's team, as it was known then. This was made up of a group of six young dogs all about one year old and presided over by Boss, a grizzled warrior of eight years, resembling an old lion, who had pulled sledges for the English in Graham Land for four years before joining the French for two years here. When you met Boss for the first time you found something indomitable about the old scarred warrior that took your heart and held it. Troby was the second of the team and was out of action through spinal paralysis. The rest were the young dogs. Seismo, a small solid little dog, who did not seem particularly remarkable at the time, but who was to be known to us later as the 'little tough.' Maru, a great shambling friendly dog, who also was to be only too

well known to us later. Then there was Astro, a great white
dog, peculiar in that the wolf hackle running the length of
his back was very prominent. And lastly Wild, a long-legged
thin-bodied dog, who attracted my attention at once by
biting my wrist in an effort to pull me back to him as I left
after patting him.

Away from them was Pickles' team, the old dogs already
mentioned. Pickles was a great handsome dog with the same
characteristics as Bjorn. He was most attached to Judy, the
bitch of the team, so much so that she was always known as
'Mrs. Pickles.' Two indescribably filthy Labrador types were
lying at the other side of the Pickles pair. Their remarkable
fur, about six inches long, made them look like baby ele-
phants. They were lying in a mass of old seal blubber and
ancient bones, and for at least an inch their fur was im-
pregnated with filth. These two were Aspirin and Hobbs,
who was sick. A particularly vicious specimen was attached
to the chain on the other side of Judy. This was a heavily
built black dog, with a distrustful and evil eye, who an-
swered to the name of Nick. The last of the team were
Bobby and Nelson, two rather peculiar animals, both of
whom had had rough treatment at some stage of their career.
Bobby was just a poor terrorized animal who at the approach of man crouched down trembling and no amount of
kindness throughout a year could remove his fear. He
seemed to take a perverted pleasure in being savagely
beaten up by Nick each day. He never made any attempt to
defend himself, or escape from Nick's onslaught, but just
rolled on his back and took an inverse sort of joy in the
savaging given him. Nelson, however, was peculiar. He was
as distrustful of men as was Bobby, but not really afraid.
He had a most curious manner of looking at you and, though
he seemed to take a certain amount of pleasure in being
patted, the moment you turned your back Nelson moved in
swiftly behind, with his teeth showing and an odd light in

his eyes. After a year of studying Nelson the conclusion was that he was a half-wit, nothing else could account for his odd actions. And by nature homicidally inclined!

Such were the three teams. Two young dogs had gone with Marret's party to Pointe Géologie, Pomme, a young edition of Aspirin, and Yacka, a silly little young bitch resembling a border collie. There were also two dogs, not yet members of teams, chained to the radio mast, Ives and Roald; and scampering about the camp free from responsibilities were two half-grown puppies, Paddy and Nanjipok. The last of the canine population were a nursing mother living with two little fluffy balls of puppies in a private kennel near the hut door. These were Sis and her two little ones.

By the time I had made the tour of the dog lines, I was hopelessly muddled. About the only two names I could remember were Boss and Aspirin; the rest seemed a mass of identical and anonymous dogs, and I despaired of ever learning all their names, let alone attaching each name to its respective dog. To aid myself in this task I drew a plan of each of the dog lines with the names attached to each dog like this—

Troby   Seismo   Astro   Boss   Wild   Maru

Which was an excellent idea, until I or someone else used the team and chained them up on the wrong chains when finished.

The next day was feeding day, for as a rule the dogs were fed once every three days. Feeding the dogs was not a very complicated affair, but to familiarize me with the technique Schwartz fed them while I looked on and gave what aid he needed. First we took a sledge and went down to the dump of dog food. This was just a frozen mass of seal carcasses. We loaded on a complete seal carcass and dragged it back to the first dog line. The moment the dogs saw what was going on they commenced to howl, though sing is a better description of the noise made by huskies. They do not bark as do normal dogs but howl like wolves. However, with twenty or so dogs howling on different notes the general effect though loud is not unpleasing, so that I choose 'singing' to describe the noise they make. The carcass was then hacked into four-pound lumps with an axe, for a knife would make no impression at all on the frozen meat. At each stroke of the axe the crescendo of noise from the dogs got higher, and they became more and more excited. In the excitement fights broke out all over the dog lines, as one dog, in his anticipation of the food to come, bit another.

As each dog's morsel was thrown to it, it dragged the meat to the furthest limit of its chain to be free from interference from the others, then fell on it like a ravenous wolf, tearing great mouthfuls loose and gulping them down, only pausing to bare its fangs momentarily at its neighbours on the chain. Any idea that these animals are just normal friendly dogs, such as we know in civilization, is immediately dispelled on watching them at feeding time.

The carcass of one full-grown Weddel seal was just enough to feed all the dogs once. That meant that to maintain the three teams for one year, something in the order of one hundred and twenty seals would have to be found, killed and the carcasses dragged back to the station.

The following day, I saw a large Weddel seal basking on the loose floes packed in the bay, just behind the station. There is no question of hunting, or of the thrill of the chase, in killing a Weddel seal. It is simply a cold-blooded and cruel assassination. For thousands of years they and their ancestors have sun-bathed in perfect peace on the pack ice, fearing no enemy at all on land; the only enemy they know is the orca or killer whale, a toothed whale up to thirty feet long, which preys on all that swims in the Antarctic waters. These whales are cruel and voracious and usually hunt in packs. They have been observed smashing pack ice by intelligent and concentrated action, rising from the depths and stabbing the floe with their great blunt heads in order to get the seals lying on it. Consequently the Weddel seal has no fear whatsoever on land, and his reaction when frightened is not to save himself by plunging into the water, but on the contrary to crawl farther away from the friendly water that could save him.

This poor unfortunate victim of the dogs' needs was lying a little way from the shore on a large block of loose floe ice. He was lying on his back sunning his underside, half asleep, quietly scratching his dappled stomach with his flippers. My approach, hopping from floe to floe, passed completely unnoticed. It was only when I prodded him with the rifle muzzle to manœuvre his ungainly body into a position where I could be sure that one shot would kill him instantly, that he opened his eyes. As he rolled over and cocked up his head to see what it was all about, he gave a little soft protesting bark at the rude disturbance of his slumbers, and after looking at me for a second or two, dropped back his head and closed his eyes. The heavy rifle bullet struck just where it should, midway between and a little lower than the two front flippers.

As I said, seal killing is a particularly cold and callous form of murder.

The next day found me using one of the teams for the first time. The commands were quite simple. '*Ee-ee!*' for 'go'; '*Heely!*' for 'right'; '*Yuck!*' for 'left'; and the familiar '*Whoa!*' for 'stop.' To emphasize the commands the driver was supplied with a twenty-foot rawhide whip, which none but a circus performer could possibly use. The efforts of the driver with this infernal weapon were, no doubt, a great source of amusement for his dogs. Nothing could be more amusing for a mischievous husky than to see an exasperated driver draw back the whip with the clear intention of giving the husky a cut where it would do the most good, and then, as usually happened, see the driver receive the thong about his own neck.

I chose Bjorn's team for the day. The work involved was quite simple. Down on the ice, near where the ship had berthed, were the carcasses of seals killed during the voyage, and dumped during landing operations. They were about five hundred yards from the station and all I wished to do was to ferry them to the dog lines. That meant a trip of five hundred yards with an empty sledge and a return trip with the sledge loaded with two seal carcasses each time. There is a catch—the empty sledge part of it, for it is then quite impossible to hold in the number of dogs needed for the loaded journey. The only time one is able to stop is when the dogs feel like doing so, and they, of course, are fully aware of the state of affairs. Dogs really do love pulling a sledge. It is to them the equivalent of being taken for a walk, and I am sure they consider it pure unrestrained fun with an empty sledge, like running free as against being taken for a walk on a leash. Coupled with this is their attitude towards the individual drivers. Until the driver has asserted himself, and proved to their satisfaction that he is in earnest and will stand no funny business, who can blame them for taking as many liberties as they dare?

With the sledge moored by a tie rope to a picket I succeeded in getting the team harnessed with no more than the ordinary number of fights, but at the time it seemed to me that I would never get the snapping and snarling beasts into their harness and under way. I loosed the tie rope and called out 'Ee-ee.'

And away we went like the wind, unfortunately in the wrong direction.

By dint of much screaming of 'Yuck!' and some rather ineffectual work with the whip, I managed to turn the team and at a flat run descended the ice slope to the dump of carcasses. Since there was, immediately after the carcass dump, an ice cliff of twenty-feet or so with particularly cold water beneath, I could not help wondering how well trained were this team and how they responded to 'Whoa!'

I need not have worried; a dump of seal carcasses was much too interesting to be passed by lightly and, without any command on my part, we pulled up against the objective. Here there was a further general squabble as the team attacked the nearest carcass. Bjorn, the big leader, immediately fell upon Fram his lieutenant, not because Fram had done anything, but just as a matter of principle. Fram like all good lieutenants took his beating lying down without any attempt to defend himself, and when it was finished squirmed on his stomach to lick Bjorn's lips in token of abject submission. Meanwhile the two inseparables, Milk and Tiki, engaged in fraternal strife until Bjorn and Fram fell upon the two of them together. Ifaut, the gentle lady, stayed completely out of the male squabbling, and profited by the diversion created by gulping down the maximum of seal meat in the minimum of time.

With two seal carcasses strapped on the sledge I began the return trip. Just beyond the dump was a small obstacle consisting of a short steep slope of blue ice on which the dogs could get little purchase and myself none at all. It was quite hard work to inch the sledge up to the top by dint of much straining of the dogs in their harness, and pushing by me at the rear of the sledge. Several times when we had almost made it the dogs would momentarily cease hauling and the heavily loaded sledge would slide back and dogs and equipment and driver found themselves in a tangle at the bottom of the slope. At last I got the dogs on to the rougher snow at the top of the slope, and was just breathing a sigh of relief, when the dogs took charge and the sledge whisked away out of my hands. I went sliding backwards to the bottom of the slope, while the dogs bounded off in high glee with the sledge behind them in the general direction of the camp. There is nothing more humiliating for a would-be dog driver than to be seen running after his sledge and team, some hundred yards behind, desperately panting and croaking 'Whoa!', while the dogs, thoroughly enjoying themselves and taking no notice at all, bound gaily ahead. I found the silly beasts with the sledge jammed against a mast lying down in their harness, with their great tongues lolling out in happy smiles, waiting my arrival. They were, no doubt, very pleased with their efforts in training their new guardian.

We were at that stage beginning to settle in for our year at Port Martin, the old party having shown us over the station and we of the new party gradually assuming the routine duties of the station. That night the ship returned to Port Martin, but was unable to come inshore because of bad weather and remained steaming up and down the bay. They announced by radio that the landing of Marret's group at Pointe Géologie had been completed and that, as soon as the weather permitted, they could come inshore to pick up the members of the old party and then sail for home. The beginning of our year at Port Martin was drawing close. Everything seemed to be going to plan.

But at 3 a.m. the following morning something happened which changed the whole plan of operations for the coming year.

I was woken by Dubois, the night duty man, rushing through the sleeping quarters crying 'Incendie!' and although my French was not very good at that stage, I had no trouble in deciding what was meant by the cry.

Slipping into a pair of trousers and a jersey and seizing a fire extinguisher en route, I hurried down the hut towards the engine room. I found the fire burning strongly in the short narrow passageway connecting the engine room with the main hut. Michel Barré, the leader of the old party, was already there.

It was hopeless. The entire engine room was an inferno and the half blizzard blowing outside was fanning the flames in great lashing tongues up the passage. There was absolutely no hope of saving the engine room or fighting the fire there. The best we could hope for was to hold the flames at the passage and so save the main hut. Barré, Dubois and I were in the narrow passage, being the first arrivals, and as there was only room for us the others passed fire extinguishers as required.

Under the concentrated output of three chemical extinguishers we could beat the flames down. But in the few seconds when the extinguishers were empty, and we felt for others behind, the wind drove the fire back, reclaiming all that we had gained. What made the position difficult was a small lean-to built against the passage. This was burning fiercely and contained the cylinders of hydrogen used for meteorological purposes. Hydrogen is highly explosive. Gradually we were forced back in the passage and finally had to retire outside and recommence the attack on the flames from above the passage by hacking a hole through the roof. Then the supply of fire extinguishers failed. Simultaneously someone announced that the main hut was now burning under the floor and filling with smoke. Accordingly, the main effort was swung from fire-fighting to salvage. Even so, there was little time. When the fire reached the main hut it was a matter of minutes. With a fifty-mile wind fanning them the flames engulfed the main hut as we watched. All that was salvaged were the scientific records of the previous

year and a few odds and ends of personal belongings. The
hungry flames consumed the rest.

All this took less than half an hour, from the first cry of
'*Incendie!*' to the moment when we all stood round in the
biting wind and watched the last wall of what had been a
first class Antarctic base collapse into the white heat of the
ashes. In half an hour Port Martin had virtually ceased to
exist. All that remained of the station was a small emergency
hut known as the 'refuge hut' and several small huts round
about which were used as instrument shelters.

Schwartz had thoughtfully liberated the dogs who were
threatened by the flames. They were wandering about the
outskirts of the fire too impressed by the magnitude of the
flames to indulge in their usual amusement of fighting among
themselves.

Everyone huddled into the tiny refuge hut to escape the
cold, keen wind outside. The three weasels, the mechanical
transport of the station, were parked away from the hut and
so had been spared in the general catastrophe. In them were
their wireless sets, so while the new party members held a
conference to decide whether they could stay on or not, the
old members made radio contact with the ship and told them
of the extent of the disaster.

In the cramped confines of the refuge hut, gulping down
steaming coffee, the new party discussed the problem of the
coming year. Garcia, our leader, after considering all the
arguments, gave his decision. The party would re-embark for
France on the *Tottan* immediately. Except for that which
could be salvaged quickly in the next few hours the station
would have to be temporarily abandoned. The ship would
call at Pointe Géologie and advise Marret of what had happened to give him the chance of re-embarking for France or
staying on.

It must be remembered that Marret's little base, though
self-contained, was not designed to operate alone, but under

the protective wing of the strong base at Port Martin, and that protecting wing had been rudely lopped off. So it was considered that Marret, too, would be forced to abandon his base until the following year.

The dogs presented a problem with only two solutions, either to take them on the ship or shoot them all immediately. To enter Australia (a way-stop on the trip to France) with a group of huskies is very difficult, because of quarantine laws, but to give the poor animals a chance of survival it was decided to load them on the ship. Two sick dogs, Troby and Hobbs, were to be shot.

The men worked non-stop from the moment the ship pulled in to the ice cliff until it sailed for Pointe Géologie some eight hours later. All available stores immediately on hand near the beach-head were loaded on to the ship. But it was rather a haphazard selection, for most of these stores were the new year's supply and had not been grouped or sorted.

I have mentioned our three weasels. A weasel is a tracked vehicle resembling the Army Bren gun carrier, which the French had been using during the past two years as a means of mechanical transport both on the sea ice and on the Polar Plateau. These three vehicles were run up on a rocky exposure and closed down. They were left there to be salvaged by a later expedition.

Last to go aboard were the dogs. They were led in pairs down to the ship on their chains and, despite their frightened struggling, unceremoniously hauled on board. I was supervising this, and all my carefully memorized names in respect to place in their teams went by the board, thus the teams became hopelessly mixed on the foredeck. At regular intervals the deck became a seething dog fight. The last team to come on board was Pickles'. In this team was Hobbs, one of the two to be shot. Poor old Hobbs, he realized that something was wrong. All the others were highly excited at the prospect of something unusual happening, but not so Hobbs. He sat back on his haunches and howled; a deep mournful howl that fitted in well with the desolate surroundings and the ashes of the burnt-out station. Each time I came to the team I took away two dogs, but left Hobbs, whose howling became progressively more despairing, until at last all were gone and Hobbs remained alone.

My last impression, as I left Port Martin, was of the desolate twisted ruins of the station showing black against the snow and the howling of Hobbs like a lost soul, the only sound in the place. Then there was a shot and the silence of the dead descended on Port Martin.

Once aboard I checked that all was well with the dogs before turning in. All was well, especially with Aspirin who had managed somehow to work himself loose and had found a pleasant station just outside the galley door. When I found him, he was reaping the results of his enterprise. Every sailor passing to and from the mess deck gave the old reprobate a pat and something to eat. He had already reached a state of repletion but that did not worry Aspirin. Like a guest at a Roman banquet, he relieved his charged stomach and returned to the task.

For all the older dogs this voyaging by ship was old stuff, they simply found the most sheltered corner in reach of their chains and curled up. But for the young dogs, who had never seen anything but ice and an occasional outcrop of rock, the water rushing past the side of the ship was fascinating. They spent most of the trip with their front paws on the bulwards watching the water intently.

The little ship was crowded with men as well as dogs. I found a bare section of deck in one of the cabins, spread a sleeping-bag and lost interest in proceedings for the next eighteen hours. When I awoke we were lying at anchor off Pointe Géologie, and the rubber pontoon raft was bumping alongside, being loaded with stores. On going on deck I found that Marret had decided to stay on at Pointe Géologie, and all that could be of use to him there that was on board the ship was being rafted ashore. Marret offered me a post with his party which I accepted, and two others of the new Port Martin party, who otherwise would have been going back to France, also were to stay.

The picture for the coming year gradually resolved itself. Seven men, Marret, Prévost, Rivolier, Duhamel, Vincent, Lépineaux and myself would be staying the year. Most of the dogs would be landed at Point Géologie, not so much in the hope that any serious work could be done with them but just to give them a chance of survival. At Pointe Géologie there was only one broken-down sledge and practically no harness. But the place teemed with life, mostly birds and penguins, but also seals, so the chance of finding enough seal meat for the dogs for the year was good.

The ship did not stay long at Géologie. The season was well advanced and it was necessary to clear the area as early as possible, before the sea froze over for another year. It took only about four hours in all for Marret to make his decision and then to clear the holds of anything that might be of use to us in the coming year. All on board who would be returning gave their personal clothing to equip Pointe Géologie, where even this was in short supply.

On shore, since being landed, Marret's group had already begun erecting a hut. Three small polar tents were standing near the hut and these provided shelter until the hut could be completed. Food and equipment cases were dumped on the exposed rocks. A considerable quantity was still lying on the edge of the pack ice half a mile from the hut site. It was here that we seven stood and watched the last boat chug away to the ship and be taken on board. Then with a hoot of the ship's siren the *Tottan* steamed away to the north, out of our lives and towards Australia and eventually France, leaving us seven standing grouped at the edge of the ice floe.

At this stage we did not even have a radio set capable of making contact with the world outside, and seven men seemed a very small world indeed in the vastness of the Antarctic.

The dogs were chained in a continuous line along the rock outcrop opposite the camp. At the top was Boss's team, next Bjorn's, while Pickles' team was still tied to odd stores at the waterfront with us. As there was a heavy sledge load to be towed up to the camp the easiest solution was to attach the team by their chains and drive them up to the camp towing the sledge behind them. All the dogs save Aspirin found this quite a good idea, but poor Aspirin paid the price of his continual gluttony on board and was violently sick every yard of the journey. As I chained them up in their new lines Aspirin wore a sad and dreamy look, for his thoughts were still with the *Tottan* and its warm and hospitable galley.

If we could offer the dogs nothing else, they had, from the moment they opened their eyes, one of the finest views in the world. Immediately below them was a stretch of unbroken bay ice, dotted with little hurrying groups of Adelie penguins and the shapeless forms of seals. Behind that was a great and tranquil bay studded with little icebergs of fantastic shapes, the water showing indigo blue under the light of the midnight sun. Behind the bay and blotting out all the visible horizon was the imposing tongue of the Terra Nova glacier. Its crevasses and caves glowed with sapphire blues and emerald green and the white snowfield was tinged with blue shades from the low but never setting sun. Whisks of filmy cirrus cloud, like windblown feathers, lazed across the azure sky.

Quite by chance, we seemed to have found a little Antarctic paradise. Perhaps that was why the Emperor penguin made its home there, and the many little islands scattered over the bay made nesting grounds for thousands of Antarctic birds. There are few corners in this grim and desolate land, mantled as it is with perpetual ice and snow, that offer such a sanctuary. Port Martin, on the contrary, was a god-forsaken place. Sir Douglas Mawson, the Australian Antarctic explorer, made his base at Cape Denison, sixty miles to the east of Port Martin. He wrote a book on his two years' stay in Adélie Land, and called it very appropriately *The Home of the Blizzard*. By his and French records, Adélie Land can be claimed, without fear of contradiction, the windiest place in the world. This never-ending wind, sweeping down from the Antarctic plateau accompanied by the prevailing low temperatures, makes a year of work in Adélie Land an experience to be remembered with a reminiscent shudder.

I will attempt to describe Adélie Land. The southern continent is a roughly circular mass of land approximately bordered by the Antarctic circle with two great indents—the Ross and Weddel Seas. A long peninsula juts up from the continent almost reaching Cape Horn; this is the Graham Land Peninsula. The whole area is larger than that of North America. Except for small rock outcrops and the tops of mountain ranges a deep icecap shrouds the whole continent. The thickness of this ice is generally believed to be about two thousand feet. In Adélie Land we had it about 1,800 feet thick. In summer, except in certain areas, the open sea laps against the coastal ice cliffs for a few months. For the rest of the year a belt of many hundreds of miles of frozen sea and drifting pack ice forms about the continent, isolating it from the rest of the world until the following summer. Adélie Land is the French sector of the continent, being that part of it bounded by the 136th and 145th meridians of longitude from the coast to the South Pole where, of course, all meridians meet.

It was first discovered by the French explorer Dumont d'Urville who touched the continent near Pointe Géologie in 1840. Since then, in 1911, Sir Douglas Mawson had visited

Adélie Land and worked there for two years, and after that it had not known men until the present French expedition set up their station at Port Martin in 1949.

There are several rocky outcrops at the coast, a few islands, and the rest is perpetual ice. An ice cliff, two hundred feet high, marks the coast, behind which the ice rises gently and regularly to the Pole. At sixty miles inland one finds oneself at three thousand feet altitude, without ever consciously mounting a hill or a mountain. The ice slope just undulates, completely featureless except for the glacier valleys near the coast, and as one marches southward there is always a gentle upward slope and a crest ahead which, once reached, just gives a further gentle upward slope and another crest ahead. More desolate than any desert is the Polar plateau in blank unchanging whiteness.

There is practically no soft snow in Adélie Land. The ever present wind cuts it and shapes it into waves known as sastrugi and compacts it as hard as marble. In other places the snow never has a chance to stay and the blue ice of the ice cap is, at the surface, as smooth and hard as polished glass. The dogs go crazy with delight when there is a fall of normal snow that stays soft a day, gambolling in it like kittens, plunging their noses deep into its softness and throwing it in the air and playing with the clouds of snow that they have made. In Adélie Land such a phenomenon is rarer than rainfall in the centre of Australia.

So there is this great icy slope descending from the South Pole to the coast near the Antarctic circle in a massive featureless shield, and near the coast there are the rivers of the icecap, the glaciers of faster moving ice pushing their long snouts up to fifty miles from land. And prevailing over this desolate land is the ruling divinity, the blizzard. Blizzard, blizzard, and more blizzard.

The reader might well ask what is 'blizzard'? It is a rather loose term misused a great deal when describing a cold

tempest. Its sense is best defined as in the glossary of Mawson's book—'A high wind at low temperatures accompanied
by drifting, but not necessarily falling, snow.' When the wind
beats up above seventy miles per hour and the drift becomes
so intense that visibility is no more than a yard or so, then,
in Adélie Land, one begins to consider it a blizzard. Anything less is merely drifting snow. Marret, who had spent a
previous year at Port Martin, saw snow falling vertically
once, at all other times it was sheeting by horizontally.
Everything else in this majestic and impressive land becomes
insignificant before the fury of this awe-inspiring force.

Such is Adélie Land. And such are the conditions in which
my friends the dogs worked willingly and happily.

Before giving too ugly a picture of this land I must repeat
that at Géologie we had found a little sheltered corner. And
frequently, when the blizzard raged visibly on all sides of us,
for some reason the few square miles at Géologie were
spared. Why this should be is hard to say, but probably it
was due to the shape of the plateau behind us. Whatever the
reason, we had local weather much better than that known
to prevail in the rest of Adélie Land.

Strictly speaking the camp was not at Pointe Géologie,
but built on the Ile des Pétrels, the largest of a group of
islands in the bay, and situated about half a mile from land.
Pointe Géologie was a separate rocky cape about four miles
away across the bay. Just behind us was another cape known
as the Nunatak du Bon Docteur and all about us were other
islands. The whole little archipelago was situated in a deep
bay made up by the glacier tongue to our east and the northward coastline to the west. Because of its favoured climate
and the great quantity of exposed rock of the islands and the
capes, this bay gave sheltered homes to all known forms of
Antarctic birds and nesting ground for the seals in summer.

In winter—the Antarctic winter—the birds and seals leave
and disappear away to the north and the land becomes

sterile and lifeless. Even the Adelie penguin finds winter in the Antarctic too grim for him. But there is one animal that stays. Pointe Géologie is the fourth known Emperor penguin rookery in the world. Though the rest of the Adélie coast may be lifeless throughout the winter, at Géologie we have the Emperor penguin in his thousands throughout the dark cold winter. It was to study this peculiar and primitive bird that the little base of Ile des Pétrels had been set up.

Just before making his historic dash to the Pole, Captain Scott sent a small party of three men from Cape Royds to Cape Crozier, a distance of sixty miles, to bring back some eggs of the Emperor Penguin. This journey, so well described by the only surviving member of the party, Apsley Cherry-Garrard, in his *Worst Journey in the World,* was to become one of the epics of Antarctic exploration. His two companions, Wilson and Bowers, were to perish with Scott a few months later in the return from the South Pole. Why was this little journey of sixty miles to become history and be described with justification as the worst journey in the world? Mainly because it was made in the depth of the Antarctic winter. For the first time men ventured forth into the incredibly cold night of the Antarctic winter and went on a journey, and, more important, after accomplishing their mission under almost impossible conditions returned alive to their base. When one considers that only a few years before this, men seriously disputed whether it was possible for a party in a warm well-equipped hut to winter in the Antarctic, one begins to realize the magnitude of the accomplishment.

But why was not the journey made in the more clement conditions of the summer, a reasonable man might well ask. Unfortunately, the Emperor penguin is not a reasonable bird, and in that lies a great deal of interest. It chooses to lay its egg in mid-winter under conditions in which no other animal could survive, let alone raise its young. And if Wilson, Bowers and Cherry-Garrard wanted Emperor penguin eggs, they had no alternative but to set out in winter on their search.

We, of the Ile des Pétrels, were to be privileged in that, not half a mile from our hut, was a rookery of twelve thousand Emperor penguin. For the first time men were to be able to watch a complete year of the life of this primitive and peculiar bird. It was for this reason that the little base had been planned, and the most important phase of the work ahead was to make this study as complete as possible.

So once the work on the hut was complete we assembled our meagre resources and waited the arrival of the Emperors.

2

Early Days and Maternity Problems

The first problem with the dogs was raised by Prévost, the biologist. He was charged with a study of the animal and bird life in the area and naturally enough did not want the dogs roaming loose assassinating his specimens. Already we had seen how quickly they could dispose of an Adelie penguin and had no doubts that they were equally efficient in killing any other form of life. To protect his flock, Prévost demanded that all dogs should be kept chained securely. So the first serious task was to build escape-proof chains. It sounds easy enough to chain a dog so that he cannot escape, but as it turned out the ingenuity of the whole seven of us was to be severely taxed for the rest of the year.

Because Prévost was more or less patron of the defenceless wild life and I was the captain of the enemy, there was always a professional, or rather technical, state of enmity between us. There was nothing personal in it. For his part I was the rather insecure thread holding up the sword of Damocles, and for my part he was the reason why my poor dogs could not be let loose to have a glorious scamper over the island.

The new dog lines took a day to complete and I was quite sure that they would be sufficient. The basis was a ½ in. steel wire cable anchored at each end on to steel pickets drilled into solid rock. The individual chains were knotted on the

cable at intervals, and each dog was clipped on to his chain
with either a heavy dog-clip, or a mountaineer's safety clip.
The dogs had only been attached to the new lines for a day
when Jackie Duhamel called out that Maru, one of the young
dogs, had just slipped his collar and had disappeared in the
direction of the Adelie penguin rookery, just behind the
camp. I departed in hot pursuit with a whip. By the time I
arrived, there was a trail of dead penguins leading through
the rookery and at the head of the trail Maru, killing penguins with savage efficiency, not to eat but just out of the
sheer joy of killing.

When he saw me, he took to flight and began to play hide-
and-seek in the rookery, but even with me panting along a
few yards behind him, cutting him occasionally with the lash
of the whip, he still found time to pause a second to seize a
penguin by the throat. When I finally recaptured him, Prévost had counted 150 dead penguins as a result of less than
a quarter of an hour's work.

Maru thus achieved the first rating as a public enemy but,
alas, he was to be joined by many others before the year was
out.

In this early period the dog team in use was mainly
Bjorn's. In intellectual capacity poor Bjorn would have had
difficulty in achieving the status of a half-wit, but he was the
strongest dog we possessed and had made himself undisputed leader of his team. His only interest in life was pulling
and, from the moment he was put in harness to the moment
he was taken out, he pulled. But mental problems such as
what to do when a command was given were always too
much for him. It was not that he did not try to understand.
He tried ever so hard. There were only three possible courses
of action on receipt of a command from the driver, to turn
left, to turn right or to stop. The rest of the team would
generally start to veer off in the proper direction but on seeing their leader heading off in the opposite one they would

swing round and follow him. At this I would scream with
rage and Bjorn would realize that he was wrong. He would
then usually stop to consider the problem, only to be bumped
by Fram his lieutenant swinging in behind him. This gave
him an opportunity to save face as he fell on Fram and beat
him up for heading in the wrong direction. Fram, when this
was over, turned round on the twins, Milk and Tiki, and
gave them a small beating by way of passing on the reproof.
Ifaut, the intelligent and beautiful bitch of the team, would
be standing at the end of her trace apart from the others,
facing in the required direction, throwing a glance of contempt at her blundering menfolk. On seeing Ifaut, a wave
of understanding would dawn on Bjorn and he would bound
off, throwing a sideways nip at Fram in passing.

One trouble with Bjorn's team at that time was the presence of two bitches, Ifaut and Helen. When dogs fight it
is more or less a gentlemanly affair, ears may be torn off, legs
bitten and opened to the bone, and great cutting slashes
made in the body, and the whole affair is passed off among
them as a harmless way of livening up an otherwise dull
morning and finishes as it began with no ill feeling on either
side. But when the bitches fight it is a different affair altogether. It is a brave man who attempts to break up a fight
between two females. They become bloodthirsty little
bundles of snapping fury; it is very much a personal affair
and every bite is carefully placed where it hurts the most.
What male could have found such an excruciatingly painful
bite as seizing one's opponent by the upper lip under the
nose and worrying it, which was Helen's favourite tactic. I
think Helen, the little black beast, realized she was not so
well endowed with feminine charms as Ifaut her rival and
at every opportunity did her best to destroy Ifaut's attrac-
tiveness. Although Helen was usually the original aggressor
the gentle and beautiful Ifaut, when once aroused, also

adopted such purely feminine tactics with equally vicious results.

It is not because of any sense of gallantry that the dogs never fight with bitches; they know that a hundred-pound dog in his prime is completely outclassed by an eighty-pound bitch even when she is feeling a little out of sorts.

Helen, on the other hand, was such a perfect little fiend that she could not stay out of any form of strife, and whenever the dogs were fighting, Helen was always in the thick of it, biting indiscriminately to keep the dispute going at high tempo if it showed any signs of flagging. But never, even in the most excited state in the middle of a general brawl, did any dog dare to put fangs to Helen. They all knew that the little black bitch was much too dangerous.

But the position, as far as the team went, was becoming impossible, and it became necessary to leave one of the two bitches out of the team on each sortie, otherwise too much time was spent separating the two females in their jealous wrangling.

Milk and Tiki were a strange pair. They were quite inseparable and had to be considered as one unit and not as two separate dogs. The attachment was more like that of a husband and wife and Tiki seemed to hold the 'feminine' role in the partnership and in the dog lines bullied Milk, the stronger of the two, unmercifully and peevishly, stealing Milk's food quite shamelessly, and generally behaving as though he knew Milk, in his affection, would let Tiki do what he pleased. However, once in the team with the other dogs, it was Milk who did the fighting for the pair; Tiki was terrified of Bjorn and Fram, but not so Milk who, though soundly trounced by both Bjorn and Fram, both collectively and individually at frequent intervals, was never known to make the routine play of submission to his leader that was usual and which spared the dog continual attacks from the leader. Tiki, on the other hand, screamed with terror and fell on the ground on his back the moment any other dog came near him. And without Milk, he remained in a state of continual terror. Together in the team always, they were also a source of continual annoyance to the driver; they were continually changing from side to side of each other and tangling their traces.

The last member of the team was a new addition from Boss's team. It was Maru, the terror of the penguin rookeries, who, apart from being continually bullied by Bjorn and Fram, seemed happy enough in this new team. Maru's great quality was that he always minded his own business, and was always so interested in penguins that he never gave trouble either to the driver or to Bjorn. The thing that surprised me most was that of all the dogs Maru, the already convicted penguin killer, seemed to be the favourite of Prévost the biologist. The reason perhaps was that Maru's lust for killing penguins was so evident that Prévost, once having accepted it, could not take the very real danger to his birds seriously. Maru, watching penguins, was a caricature of Disney's Big Bad Wolf looking at the fat little pigs. His eyes would follow every move of the penguin he was watching, his great tongue would roll round his mouth in the ecstacy of anticipation and a dreamy reminiscent light would show in his eyes. Even running with the team on the sea ice, he never let himself be fully taken up with the business of pulling like the others. As the team passed a group of penguins five would still be running straight ahead, and one dog, Maru, would be pulling away at right angles in the direction of the penguins. A sharp call of 'Maru!' and without enthusiasm he would take up again his position in the team.

As Prévost said, 'You must admit at least that he's obedient.'

In that early period the half-grown puppy Roald became rather my pet. Being too young to take a place in a team, he was tied at the end of the dog lines with the six-months-old bitch Yacka. Thus the two youngest played together as do all young things. As Roald showed no interest in the penguins, except a timorous attempt at play, Prévost gave approval for his accompanying me on walks, and quite often took him himself on his daily rounds of the rookeries. Actually he was not a very appealing dog, being rather ugly in build and colouring and sillier in behaviour than was justified by his lack of age. The other dogs always chained in the lines regarded his carefree freedom as a form of favouritism and took great pleasure in lying in wait until the gambolling Roald came within reach of their chains. Then there would be a scuffle, some startled yelps and Roald would be seen streaking for the hut, his tail between his legs, while the aggressor yawned in a pleased fashion before going to sleep again. Perhaps the most severe shock for Roald was when his little playmate, Yacka, first became strangely beautiful to the other dogs. The old grizzled warrior Boss, who through long experience never missed such an opportunity, wasted no time in breaking his chain and joining Yacka. Roald, returning from a walk saw his playmate Yacka and the tough old Boss apparently playing together. Deserting me, he bounded off to join in the fun. He bounded round and round the two, barking and prancing, but to his annoyance neither Boss nor Yacka took the least notice of him. Feeling peeved, he gave Boss a sharp nip on the back leg.

Perhaps it would be kindest to draw a veil over what followed. Boss looked round with a look of stunned astonishment and he fell on Roald like a flash of lightning. Yacka too, vexed by the interference, joined Boss in the attack. Roald only just saved himself by fleetness of foot from complete destruction. He spent several days under the hut after this episode, trying to understand what change had come over his little friend Yacka.

One time I was walking with Roald at the end of the bay ice. A penguin took fright and made for the water at top speed, and Roald bounded after it, also at top speed. At the water's edge Roald did not slow down, for he did not understand water; he had never seen anything but ice and snow, and an occasional piece of rock. He travelled many yards over the surface, carried by his own momentum, before disappearing. He came to the surface a mass of flailing legs and managed to scramble part way on to a block of loose floe ice. And there he howled, making no attempt to save himself, but just howled desperately for help like a baby that has suddenly hurt itself. He was never seen to go near water again. He was beginning to learn that life is not all scamper and tail-wags.

One of the things that had to be done urgently was to lay in a stock of seal meat for the dogs and also to supplement our own slender food supply, for, though we were seven, our food supply was only for three. Although we were all busily engaged finishing the hut, whenever seals were seen we had to release one or two men to kill, dress and collect them. As the dogs were my responsibility, I was usually chosen, and Prévost, who wanted seal for his biological work, usually helped me. The reason for this haste was that in a short time the last of the bay ice would break out and we would find ourselves on a very small island. The only seals that would be available to us would be the occasional ones that hauled up on the island itself. Further, once the sea froze over again it would freeze solid to the horizon and our seals would desert us for the winter months. It was imperative to lay in a good supply of seal meat before winter closed down on us.

One day there were sixteen seals spotted on the bay ice just below us. George Lépineux hurried down on foot with the carbine, while I harnessed up the dogs. As usual, as I appeared from the hut with whip and dog harnesses over my shoulder pandemonium broke out. Every dog was leaping at the end of his chain clamouring to be taken. Every dog, that is, except one. Fram, lieutenant of Bjorn's team, was so incurably lazy that he looked upon a jaunt with a sledge, even on the remunerative and delightfully bloody business of killing seals, as an unjustified interruption of his slumbers.

The first move was always to attach the sledge by a leg rope to something solid before putting any dog in harness. For failing this precaution, I would hear an excited howling and sledge and lead dogs would whip past at the gallop while I was getting the last dogs ready.

The first harnessed would be Bjorn, who always claimed this right, as the leader. He would make a tour of inspection of the sledge, lifting his leg against it to show his contempt for all things human. The next was usually Ifaut, who would fawn with Bjorn for a moment, then start pulling in the direction of the hut. Fram followed, falling on his stomach and licking Bjorn's lips as token of submission; Bjorn always asserted his leadership with a few heavy growls and a snap or two. Fram then would wait until the next dog, usually Maru, arrived, and would immediately attack. Bjorn, excited by the noise, would turn on Fram again, and Maru, in saving himself, usually managed to give Fram a sharp nip. Milk and Tiki had to be brought over together, since Tiki became so terrified alone.

All the dogs now being harnessed, I should have been able to leave, but several of them had made a tour round the sledge, tangling up their traces and that had to be sorted out. Before loosing the anchor rope, a call of 'Ee-ee, les chiens!' and the dogs bounded out to the end of their traces.

A second call, the leg rope out, and away we went, the dogs wild with excitement and for the moment quite uncontrollable, with the driver hanging to the steering handles like grim death.

Just at the point where the land-based ice joined the floating bay ice is the tide crack, forming a miniature ice cliff five feet or so high. The dogs took this at the gallop, and the sledge and driver followed, the latter gripping the steering handles and hoping the sledge would land on its runners and not turn over in mid-air. I slipped at the shock of the sledge striking the ice and fell off but managed to grab the end of the runner with one hand. A group of penguins attracted the dogs' attention and the sledge shot away while I dragged along behind, vainly trying to get aboard and at the same time screaming 'Whoa!' at the heedless dogs. Somehow I managed to scramble aboard and found we had already passed the first group of penguins and were heading for a second. The scattered members of the first lot were vigorously protesting such cavalier treatment, but I was glad to see no blood had been shed. Uncoiling the whip I then tried to assert myself as master, but by that time were were so close to the second group of penguins that nothing short of an atomic bomb would have turned the team. From the dogs' point of view this was glorious fun and well worth the beatings they knew must inevitably follow. They arrived in the group of penguins rather like a torpedo hitting its mark. Fortunately for the penguins, this form of attack was usually harmless as each dog had his eye on a different bird and there was too much confusion to concentrate on the job in hand. Besides, behind them was the sledge. At one time or another each had been run down by the sledge and they always made sure that they were moving forward at sufficient speed to keep ahead of it. It was impossible to do justice to a penguin without being hit by the sledge.

I must have covered most of the bay that morning before we finally arrived at the first seal. It had been a mad, uncontrolled scamper from one group of penguins to the next. On the swift surface with an empty sledge I was quite helpless to punish the villains no matter how much I might have wished to do so. The moment I let go of the sledge brake to go up to the culprit, away would go the sledge. Finally we did arrive at the first seal, already killed by Georges, and the dogs stopped and flopped on the snow, gulping down great mouthfuls to quench their thirst, and looking at me in innocent amazement.

It was rather a gruesome day. I had a dozen big seals to skin and dress and had to cart the carcasses and hides with blubber attached back to the dog food depot at the camp. Fortunately I was wearing an old set of clothes that Schwartz, the last year's dog man, had passed on to me.

The predatory skua gulls which were still with us at that time had a field day. Incredibly cheeky, these voracious birds would be pecking away at one end of the seal while I was working at the other and, apart from watching both me and the dogs warily, showed no fear at all. From time to time I would throw the axe, the steel or the knife at them to chase them away; but they would just rise into the air sufficiently to avoid the missile, then follow it and peck it just in case it was good to eat. The dogs showed no interest in them; as far as they were concerned the skuas could have flown off with the whole carcass.

Bjorn annoyed me that day. He bullied the other dogs unmercifully, particularly Fram. Having already eaten far too much, he certainly had no interest in eating more, but it seemed to hurt him to see the others enjoying themselves. If I threw a morsel of meat to Fram, Bjorn would drop on him like a thunderbolt, take his meat and drop it in a crevasse nearby. The others became terrified to touch anything with Bjorn looking on. He behaved like a great, silly, good-natured bully, not so much to torment the others but to show what a big strong fellow he was. As for patting one of the other dogs, it was quite out of the question. Bjorn would move in, with his fangs bared and a deep growling rumble issuing from his formidable jaws, and the other dog would cringe away to the shelter of the sledge. No amount of beating will ever break a leader of this habit. They are very obedient up to a point, but brook no interference in their rights over their team, considering themselves the medium between the driver and the rest of the team. Bjorn would take a rap across the muzzle, duck a second, but still continue his attack.

The sledge was awash with blood before the day was out, and left a red trail across the bay to the camp. I was in no better state. It seemed to me that I would never be able to get rid of the taste and smell of blood, blubber and dogs. My French friends informed me that I would not, I would merely get used to it! Even the dogs looked at me in mute admiration, but the final accolade was given when I was hailed as a brother by the incredibly filthy Aspirin. There was nice fried seal liver for tea that night, and though normally one of my favourite dishes it seemed to stick in my throat.

Prévost was busy at the time with a study of the giant petrels who had their nests on the rocks about the camp. Their chicks were sitting in the nests, nearly fully grown, but still unable to fly. Prévost had just finished a tour of the nests, ringing each chick with an aluminium band for identification. After tea, on coming out of the hut I was horrified to see Ifaut at the door instead of being firmly chained. I feared the worst and found that at the nearest of the giant petrel nests was a rather battered chick uttering its last squawks on this earth. By the time I got to it, it had given a convulsive shudder and lay still. I picked it up, put it back on its nest hoping it might recover. It didn't. It was very dead. And it was only too apparent how it had met its fate.

Prévost seemed quite puzzled the next morning as to how so young a thing had left its nest, gone for a walk all by itself, and unfortunately gone too close to one of the chained dogs. It was all very sad.

The skua gulls began to be a menace. The predatory and voracious gulls had found the seal meat depot, and before long there were some fifty of them pecking away at the carcasses every morning. Ten skuas can pick a carcass clean in a day or two. A counter attack was launched with the shot-gun and carbine. In the first surprise of our assault enemy casualties were heavy, and, as the skua makes fine eating, our table benefited. But despite a half dozen killed every day, their numbers increased as word passed through the skua world that there were good pickings to be had at Pointe Géologie. As it was impossible for us to maintain a continuous watch over the depot, the skuas soon learned to take to the air when a man came out with a gun in his hands, only to return as soon as he was gone.

My first solution to the problem was to take the two youngest dogs, Roald and the bitch Yacka, and chain them at the seal meat depot, working on the assumption that the depredation by two dogs should be considerably less than that of fifty marauding skuas. Yacka and Roald gorged themselves on seal meat until their straining sides could hold no more. This done, they fell asleep. The skua gulls suffered no interruption at all in their feeding habits. For both dogs and skuas it seemed such a beautiful world that it should not be spoilt by any unpleasantness from either side.

The only thing to do was to continue the attack with the shot-gun, but as cartridges were not plentiful a minimum bag of four skuas per cartridge was laid down as standing orders. Since the two dogs were still at the depot, every time someone grabbed the gun and stalked down there I expected that the bag per cartridge would be four skuas and two dogs.

The day came when the hut was officially opened and the tents we had been living in since landing, struck. It was a little hut at the time, twelve feet by eighteen feet, in which seven of us slept, lived, cooked and worked. There was not a great deal of room, and the only privacy was when one was asleep in one's bunk, and even that was liable to be violated by the foot of the man in the bunk above being put in one's face as he crawled out of bed. To celebrate the beginning

of hut life we threw a party. Because of our isolation we had
no guests.

The party was organized as an official affair, and before
the meal the flag of the Republic of Terra Nova, born that
day, was hoisted on a rafter of the hut. Its device a penguin
rampant on a field of snow. The President of the Republic,
Monsieur Marret, read a short address to the assembled Am-
bassadors, explaining that from that day forward work would
be carried out as it had been to date. He also decreed that
from that day henceforth the monetary system would be
abolished and nothing was to be bought or sold within the
Republic at pain of instant deportation. Private rights to
property had ceased to exist, he explained further; each
citizen had the right to the property of his fellows—as he had
discovered that very morning was already the accepted
custom, when he found Vincent had appropriated his gloves.

At this stage the Presidential address was cut short by the
serving of the first course, but the President threatened to
continue it when the meal was over.

The menu was—

> Paté de Foie Gras
> Thon à huile
> Coq au vin
> Foque Rôti
> Fruit Glacés
> Fromages
> Café Noir
> Wines: Pernod, Vin dé Alsace, Beaujolais.

The dinner was happy, but not hilarious, mainly because
of our limited alcoholic resources at the time. The question
of the depredations on the seal meat by the skuas was raised.
An unofficial war was already in progress between the Republic and the Realm of Skuas. Should it be recognized by
an official declaration? The President, remembering the

grand tactical value of surprise so well demonstrated in the last war, agreed that war should be officially declared but at the same time felt that, if a surprise attack on the skuas could be made simultaneously with the official declaration, the chance should not be missed. Accordingly a 'fougasse' was prepared, a frightful weapon consisting of a pound of gelignite loaded in a tin can followed by a charge of rock fragments. This infernal machine was installed covering the seal meat depot, and an electric lead run back to the hut where an electric exploder was installed. One of the twenty records which we possessed was put on the gramophone and played. This being the most popular of all was considered as the National Anthem. As its brassy strains rang out, the Governor read the official declaration of war, citing the numerous infringements of territorial rights, flagrant occupation of the airways, frontier incidents and despoliation of the resources of the community by the skuas. He regretted that the normal channels of diplomacy had failed and even active demonstrations of fire had failed to check the invasion, therefore he had no other alternative but regretfully to meet force with force. At the same time he pressed down the exploder. There was a magnificent explosion, cracking one window of the hut, startled skuas heading away in all directions and two enemy dead. The fougasse had not proved very lethal but it was certainly impressive. The skuas showed a marked aversion to that tune thereafter and the moment it was played on the gramophone they took to flight. It seemed that all we had to do to guard the seal meat depot was to play that tune over and over again. But like all things near perfect there was a slight catch. We couldn't stand it either!

It was quite an improvement on tent life to change into the hut. Not that the hut was by normal standards anything to boast about from the point of view of appointments. But it was a hut, tight against wind and snow, and the coal-burning stove was a pulsating heart of warmth giving life to our community of seven. A sheet of plywood on four packing-cases served as a table, and because the base had been planned for three there were only three chairs. As the weeks slipped by and the sun at midday became lower in the sky, bringing colder temperatures with its retreat north-ward, we began to extend the building program. First, by tearing down one wall, and with the aid of odd timbers collected from the ship before it left us, we extended the hut another twelve feet. This done, a shelter was built a short distance from the hut to house our equipment and gener-ating sets for electric power. To call this the engine room was overstressing its importance, as the generating equip-ment was a small gas driven battery charger, the main duty of which was to provide a source of power for our radio. The shelter had many functions, not the least of which from my point of view was that it was also planned to be the dog hospital.

The building program was finally completed, halted for-cibly by lack of materials. Still, what had been achieved was better than could normally be expected. We had a main hut of two rooms and a porch, and a shelter, and both were securely tied down with steel wire ropes drilled into the solid rock beneath the hut, to hold the huts against the assaults of the wind. Most of our stores were under cover, though the food cases were stacked on the rocks outside the hut, each pile marked with a long bamboo so that we might find it when covered with ice.

The weather was getting colder, and the wind drove swirl-ing drifts about the hut. Very little remained of the bay ice, just a narrow strip connecting us to the nearest island. We were now isolated from the Antarctic Continent half a mile away by a strip of open water. Some of the birds had already left for warmer climes.

Mrs. Pickles, otherwise Judy the bitch of Pickles' team,

was an expectant mother, and began to behave in an agitated manner. I installed her in a packing case just behind the hut. To make this maternity hospital as comfortable as possible the case was lined with coal sacks and a curtain of coal sacks hung across the open front. The case was then packed over with rocks to hold it down in the wind. When I went to bring Judy from her place in the dog lines, she headed direct for her new quarters and after a brief inspection crawled inside and made herself comfortable. An old dog, she had been through this before.

The following morning a minor blizzard was blowing, but the first pups born at Ile des Pétrels had found their way into the world. There were three of them to begin with but Judy soon reduced the number to two by eating the first. Poor little defenceless balls of fur, they were born into a hard world. Several hours later the second pup was found frozen stiff just outside the kennel. When I attempted to re-move the little dead body Judy saw it and tucked it between her legs with the sole survivor and firmly resisted any at-tempt to remove it. She was much more concerned about the dead one than for the living puppy, so the living puppy nearly followed the fate of the brother when he too was found outside white with snow and ice while Judy fran-tically tried to lick life back into the dead one. However once the dead one had been forcibly taken from her, she concentrated her energies on the last pup.

Despite the protecting sacks the drift snow swirled into the kennel. In a short time there was just a mound of snow and the faint outline of Judy underneath it. The pup was tucked between her back legs with her tail curled around him and her head pushed against him to keep him warm. In that little niche of warm fur and flesh he was safely pro-teced from the cold and wind. For the grown dogs, this was their normal life. When the wind rose and the drift snow began to sheet past, they curled up, backs to the wind, the four paws tucked about the sensitive tip of their noses, and like balls of fur went comfortably to sleep. After a few hours in a blizzard the dogs would be buried in the snow, and would remain like that until the weather improved. You could always tell when the blizzard was over, as the dogs would be seen emerging from their snow holes, shaking off the ice that had formed in their fur. Most of these dogs had been born in Adélie Land, and for them the howling blizzard and the intense cold were the rule. Curled up in a snug hole in the blizzard, they were very averse to moving until the storm was over, it was so warm and comfortable as they were. This could be dangerous. It took some time to be comfortably snowed in, but if they remained still for too long their fur froze to the ice beneath them, so that they could only release themselves by pulling out the frozen fur. The wiser and more experienced dogs were quite aware of this danger. They could be observed every three hours or so getting on their feet, shaking themselves and then curling up to sleep again. For the others, it was usual to make a tour of the dog lines, giving all the dogs a gentle kick to be sure they did not become iced in. Roald, the young pup, was a particularly bad offender. Being younger and less hardy than the older dogs, he always seemed to become miserable in a gale and would refuse to move even when kicked. Then, when the weather had cleared, he would attempt to get up and find himself imprisoned in the ice. Frightened, he would start jumping and struggling, tearing out tufts of hair by the roots.

For this reason, if for no other, dogs with no man to care for them would never be able to survive in the Antarctic. They would just become frozen to the ice and perish miserably.

Paton, Judy's pup, thrived. Being an only pup he was overfed by his mother. And being the sole pup in the camp he was outrageously spoilt by everyone as soon as he was strong enough to be taken into the hut for play. He was, as a result, a round distended stomach propped up on four inadequate legs, and for a long while only able to wriggle, for his legs were not strong enough to lift the main mass from the ground.

Helen, the little black beast, also needed a lodging in the maternity ward. I decided to install her immediately and not run the risk of having her pups born in the dog lines, where they would certainly perish. So a second case was installed and furnished.

Helen objected strongly to being removed from her team. Unlike Judy, she treated her kennel with contempt, preferring to sleep outside in the snow. What made it difficult for me was that she objected vocally, and by preference made her strongest protests from 10 p.m. to 6 a.m. Practically every other dog in the camp sympathized with her, although there were few with the endurance that she possessed in being able to howl a particularly piercing howl for eight hours without a break.

At breakfast the men would ask hopefully, 'Are Helen's little ones here yet?' And I would sadly shake my head.

Pickles got loose one night to go hospital visiting to Judy. As a mark of appreciation to his wife for the fine pup she had produced, he killed two giant petrel chicks and presented them to Judy. It was a charming family scene that met my eyes the next morning. Pickles and Judy lying side by side whilst Paton tumbled over the tattered remnants of the two birds.

Boss, grizzled old leader of the young dogs and victor of a thousand bloody battles, indulged in another fight, this time with Astro, the large white wolf-like dog, the most serious threat to his leadership in the team. Boss was finding it difficult to win his fights now. At nine, he was very old for a husky, and his teeth were in bad shape from years of chewing rock-hard frozen seal meat. Only one of his big fang teeth was in usable condition, and it is with the lightning slashes of the fang teeth that a husky does most damage; Boss had to bite at an extraordinary angle to secure results. And the old veteran was fighting less and less now and to a great extent was holding his position as leader among the big strong young dogs by pure bluff. He depended on lightning-quick assaults with a great deal of snarling and no actual biting to frighten the others, whereas in his palmier days it would have been a bloody and decisive battle that would have sent his opponent cowering away after a never to be forgotten beating. He was wise in the ways of the pack and knew he could never afford a defeat or even the semblance of one, or the whole team would fall on him together and a younger and stronger dog fight his way into his place. Consequently, though he fought rarely and only when he considered he had to fight, he fought with all the tactics learnt in a thousand battles and with a burst of fury that none of the others could display. And at the finish when the vanquished dog attempted to escape, and both victor and vanquished were panting with exhaustion, when any other dog, having won, would be content to let the loser escape, Boss would muster the last dregs of his failing strength to savage the victim as cruelly as he knew, so that at least that dog would not be ready to dispute his leadership for a while.

Each of the leaders had a special and decisive bite that once made usually ended the fight. With Bjorn it was always a raking slash above the right eye which laid open the scalp to the bone and bared the eye socket, and the resulting spurt of blood from the severed arteries blinded the opponents. There were few dogs who, once that slash had been received, considered further defence. With Boss, it was a strike sideways across the top of the snout, the sole effective fang tooth laying open the tender nerves of the nose like the cut of a razor, and though not quite so spectacular as the murderous wound left by Bjorn's master stroke, it was equally effective. You could recognize the members of both of these teams by the scars left in the favourite spot by the respective leaders; all Bjorn's team having a scar over the right eye, while Boss's showed a white line across the top of the snout.

Normally, the bloody battles between dogs are not interesting to watch, being usually a test of brute strength and savagery, but the Astro-Boss battle was different. Astro was a great white dog, heavier and taller than Boss, and at his prime, a year and half old. Along his back ran the raised hackle of the wolf. He was strength and savagery personified. Against him was the old champion Boss, failing in years, lighter and smaller and minus half his teeth, but past-master of every slash and parry of the game. Astro, the challenger, with nothing to lose and everything to gain and Boss, desperate, with all his leadership at stake.

It started over a piece of frozen seal meat, lying near Boss. Astro sneaked in to steal it, and Boss, on seeing him, growled deeply and Astro growled back and continued to advance. Boss leapt at him with one of his usual furious rushes planned to bluff Astro but, instead of recoiling as he should have done, Astro struck back, slashing down across Boss's shoulder, drawing blood and seizing and worrying. Where a less experienced dog would have attempted to pull free of the worrying jaws and had its shoulder laid bare, Boss yielded with the blow and in falling struck Astro across the snout and red blood spurted on the snow. The superior strength of the young dog told and Boss struck the ground heavily on his back and Astro shifted his grip with the swiftness of light to Boss's throat and began to worry him. These biting and holding tactics do little damage in the thick fur of the husky; the more experienced dog cuts and slashes in swift strokes that tear through skin.

Boss slowly moved his head across one of Astro's forefeet and seized the other just on the ankle joint where flesh is thin, then with a quick levering of the head against Astro's free leg sent the big heavy white dog flying through the air. Before Astro could recover, Boss jumped upon him and with swift raking bites attacked the tender underside of his enemy. Astro screamed and snarled with pain and snapped at Boss's grizzled forehead. One of Boss's ears, already torn and tattered, was laid open. Both dogs were bleeding freely and their jaws were flecked with foam and blood.

Astro shifted his grip to Boss's foreleg and as his powerful jaws closed, I could hear the bones crunch. Boss was badly hurt and rolled sideways to ease the pressure, still raking Astro with swift slashing bites. Too inexperienced to realize that he had Boss in an unbreakable hold, Astro released his grip on the leg and seized Boss by the throat once more. Boss swung his head across Astro's jaws as they closed on his throat, seized Astro by the foreleg and once more Astro was flung over on his back. Cripped by the badly mauled leg Boss was not quick enough to catch Astro in time and the two dogs met in mid air. Astro reeled back from Boss's onslaught then came leaping in again with his head low. Boss had been waiting for this move. Incredibly swiftly, he swung his body aside, and as the snarling head of the big white dog came level with his shoulder, he struck down across the muzzle and his fang tooth cut into the other dog's nose and ripped up towards his eyes.

It was the end of the fight. Squealing with pain, Astro wanted nothing more now but to flee the field of battle, and rolled on his back trying to get clear of the grizzled old leader. But Boss, despite the fact that he was panting with exhaustion and streaming blood, intended to clinch his victory. He raked the tender parts of Astro with shrewd bites, each one calculated to hurt as cruelly as possible. When Astro finally broke clear his only response to Boss's triumphant snarling was a pathetic whimpering like a hurt puppy.

Satisfied with the results old Boss sat down and licked his wounds. There was still a lot of fight left in the old dog.

After such a fight the dog owner has to patch up the wounds. These huskies tear each other horribly in fights, but they are tough citizens. Wounds that would kill or incapacitate a normal dog for months are treated by huskies as minor irritations, and after a day's rest they are ready for another fight. There is little to do in caring for their wounds. A dusting of antiseptic and in extreme cases a stitch or two to pull the open lips of a bad wound together, otherwise nature and the dog do the rest.

Astro, though defeated, had only minor flesh wounds but Boss's foreleg was more serious. The old dog was in considerable pain. Since it was beyond the capacity of a mere dog trainer, I called Rivolier, our doctor, into consultation. Boss was taken into the hut and given a thorough check and, as a bone seemed to be broken, Rivolier decided to put the paw in a plaster cast. Unlike most of the dogs Boss did not like the hut. Actually he did not like men and was uneasy alone with them. His whole life was his team. Though he tolerated me, even when I endeavoured to take him for a short walk away from the dog lines he would be miserably unhappy until he broke loose and rejoined his team.

At it was essential that he should rest, it was of no use putting him back in the dog lines where at first opportunity he would be involved in a second fight. So we decided to install the wounded warrior behind the hut in a private kennel as we had done with the two expectant mothers, Judy and Helen.

Boss seemed temporarily delighted with his new quarters. Then, after biting off a bit of his plaster cast, he took stock of his companions. His eyes lighted on Judy and her little pup tumbling over her. He seemed puzzled. Then he saw Helen. He thought for a few minutes as he licked his plaster cast. Then he must have realized what sort of a hospital this was. A maternity hospital! Jumping to his feet he began to bark furiously and indignantly. We could see that he was really worried. Nothing of that sort had ever happened to him before.

Still no pups for Helen. Then at last it happened—one night when the blizzard was sweeping about the hut. Above the wail of the wind we could still hear Helen's howling. It stopped. It was about four a.m. I struggled into my wind-proofs, pulled on fur boots and gloves and went out to see what it was all about. I found Helen nosing the first arrival in a puzzled manner but making no attempt to protect it from the driving snow. Both were outside the kennel. I put Helen in the kennel and then pushed the newborn pup into the softness of her stomach. She nosed it deeper into her fur and laid her head across the little body to keep it warm. It was very cold standing outside the kennel so I went into the hut for a few minutes to shake the snow out of my clothes and warm my numbed hands. When I returned to the ken-nel, it was empty and Helen's chain with collar still attached lying in the snow.

I began a frantic search for Helen and her pup. I went first to the dog lines, but Helen was not there. It was difficult searching for her in the drifting snow; visibility was only a few yards. I searched in the lee of the hut about the shelter and among the food stores. Still no Helen. Cursing soundly, I made a tour of the rocks about the kennel thinking she might have found a cranny in the rocks. Cold and worried I started back to the hut. As I passed the old barge full of camp refuse I heard a faint whimpering. Looking in I found Helen. She had scratched a hole among the rubbish and had given birth to five more puppies. With such a small dog six pups was more than she could handle. One was already frozen. The others were whimpering with the cold and helplessly trying to crawl close to the warmth of their mother. I picked up the surving five and raced them back to the kennel. Helen followed, frantically jumping at me to get back her little ones.

I put the first into the kennel and before I could stop her Helen seized it and was racing back to the rubbish heap with the pup in her mouth. Finally I got the mother and pups all installed in the kennel, and with her back to the opening and the pups underneath her legs, she settled down to sleep. All seemed to be well so I beat a retreat to the hut and my warm bed.

About four hours later, when I made a further inspection, I found five little bodies lying outside the kennel frozen as hard as little rocks and Helen happily asleep inside the warmth of the kennel. I decided to put her back in her team at once, and she left the kennel without a backward glance at her dead puppies. Pulling ahead of me on her lead she went directly to her place in the dog lines and began scratching for a piece of seal meat she had buried a month ago in the ice. That same afternoon she was out with the team on the bay ice, dragging back seal meat and happy to be doing so.

Helen seemed to have lost her maternal instinct. Perhaps this started at the time of her first litter two years before when, because of shortage of dogs, she had to be taken on a sledging journey with her pups almost due. She pulled her way with the team till the moment the pups were born. There was nothing that could be done for either mother or pups on the Antarctic plateau a hundred miles from the hut. The pups died and Helen was harnessed up and went on pulling.

3

The Emperors Arrive

In early March, the first Emperor penguins came back to land from the pack ice where they had been feeding during the Antarctic summer. The last of the bay ice had only just broken out when the sea gave signs of freezing up again. A scum of ice crystals lay on the surface of the water and, as the wind and current packed them into sheltered corners of the bay, they joined together and formed roughly circular pieces of ice, known technically as pancake ice. These pancakes, packing together, in turn froze to one another, and in a few protected corners, where the wind could not break them up, these groups of pancake ice formed a single sheet of ice.

The Emperor practically never sets his foot on land. He lives and feeds in the ocean and, when he clusters together with his fellows in the middle of the Antarctic winter to raise his solitary chick, he chooses not the firm land-based ice or rocky outcrops that the other birds and penguins prefer, but sites his rookery on the frozen-over sea. at Géologie, the site he had chosen was the strip of water between the nearest island and the mainland, and though during the year the group of penguins moved from one part of this area to another the rookery site, in general, remained the same. The first arrivals seemed puzzled, for the sea had not yet frozen over, and the site where they planned to lay their eggs was still open water. Accordingly they moved about the bay. One day they would be sitting on a piece of old floe ice floating in the bay, and on another occasion might be seen on an iceberg. Very rarely did they set foot on the islands.

Prévost, our biologist, was delighted. The arrival of the first Emperor penguins was the beginning of his most important work for the year. He was to have the unique privilege of being the first man to study these birds without an interruption from the moment of the arrival of the first until the last of them disappeared northward on a floe with the break-up of the sea ice the following summer.

Apart from our being at Pointe Géologie to study these birds, we were glad to see these first arrivals for another reason. Our stock of seal meat, although considerable, had to last many months, and would have to be carefully rationed. We looked forward to the Emperor penguins as a supplementary source of food during the long Antarctic winter.

The Emperor penguin is the largest of penguins. He stands three feet six inches high and can weigh over eighty pounds. Black-backed with a white front, his severe colouring is relieved by a gorget of gold on either side of the throat. By the end of March the rookery site was beginning to be occupied, and courting couples were everywhere. In mid-May the eggs are laid. At this stage the males are fat with accumulated blubber but the females are thin and look only half the size of their partners. The female lays only one large egg. No sooner is the egg laid than the female passes it over to the male, leaving him to guard it while she goes away to sea to feed. The male carries the egg on the upper side of its feet and, leaning forward, covers it with a surface of bare skin on its stomach. The male does not see her again from mid-May until the end of July. Unable to leave the rookery on account of his charge, he has no other alternative but to wait patiently the better part of three months, living on the stored-up blubber that he carried when he arrived.

The reason for this delay is that the female has to reach the open sea to find feeding grounds and, at that time of the year, the sea ice is solid for over a hundred miles. We went looking once for their feeding grounds and found that when we were 35 miles from land the Emperors were still heading northward with no sign of open water to our horizon.

Towards the end of his long wait the male grows very thin. The stored-up blubber has been consumed and he has to fight a continual battle against the mid-winter cold. From time to time one sees a male, complete with egg, shuffling his way northward from the rookery in search of his mate.

From the moment the egg is laid until the chick reaches maturity and can fend for itself, it faces a grim struggle for survival against two great enemies, cold and hunger. There is an enormous mortality, as one would expect in an animal which raises its young under the cruellest conditions in the world. When Wilson, Bowers and Cherry-Garrard finally won through to Cape Crozier after a bitter and terrible struggle against frightful conditions, they found the Emperor penguin rookery beneath the cliffs at Cape Crozier on the sea ice. They were surprised to find, in a rookery that was known to comprise thousands of birds, only 79 surviving chicks. Other chicks were dead and frozen in the cracks in the sea ice. They witnessed squabbles between grown birds for possession of chicks and eggs; more often than not the chick was killed by the squabbling birds driven by their intense maternal instinct. Wilson concluded that a large part of the mortality was due to these battles between grown penguins for possession of the chicks.

We were to learn, as the year progressed, that this quarrelling for chicks and eggs was only a passing phase, and that the reaction from intense maternal acquisition to outright neglect was only a matter of a month or so. Graphs drawn by Prévost of the weights and feeding times of selected chicks throughout the year identified the true killer. Hunger!

And when through slow starvation the chick weakened, the cold and wind of the next blizzard gave him a merciful release.

When one considers the truly frightful conditions prevailing in mid-winter in the Antarctic, intense cold, high winds and the nearest source of food the open sea, scores of miles away at the best, the wonder of it is not that there is a high mortality, but that any of the chicks survive at all. The eggs are laid in winter because this provides the only means of continuing the species. For, if the eggs was laid in the summer months, with the slow life cycle of the Emperor penguin, the half-grown chicks would be released to face the Antarctic winter alone. So the eggs are laid in winter. The chick is thus protected by its parents in the most difficult months and first goes out into the world alone in the middle of summer, when it has many months of reasonable conditions before the cold fury of winter once more lashes this desolate land.

The grown Emperor is one of the best adapted animals in the world for the difficult conditions in which it lives. Though mortality of chicks is high, that of the grown birds is almost nil. That is of course on land, for at sea no doubt he falls prey to the voracious sea leopard and the terrible killer whale. In a year of association with a rookery of twelve thousand birds, I only saw one adult bird dead from either hunger, exposure or plain old age.

For all living things in the Antarctic, including man, there are only two real problems, food and warmth; everything else is secondary. The living creature must be sufficiently well insulated to withstand the intense cold and must find food to produce enough heat to replace that lost. At the same time, the creature must be sufficiently unencumbered by its reserves of food and insulation to be able to move freely in its chosen medium. Granted these conditions, the creature, be it man, animal, or bird, will survive and then is only subject to accident comparable with normal risks in other more clement parts of the world.

The Emperor penguin, no doubt, evolved from a creature resembling a conventional bird. Its chosen medium became the sea and its medium for raising its young the frozen surface of that sea. The bird-like wing atrophied until they took the form of bony flippers, quite useless for flying but ideally shaped for swimming either on top of the water or beneath it, whilst the body became heavier and more streamlined. The normal fluffy feathers of a bird became a tight-packed coat of feathered quills, quite impervious to water, and the legs shortened, becoming stumpier to give less distance for the blood to circulate and exposing less surface for the loss of heat to its frozen surroundings. The blood supply became enormous in comparison with its size, so that the whole squat frame coursed with rapid flowing, warm, life-giving blood. The thick coat of primitive feathers insulated the warm, living body from the bitter wind of the Antarctic winter.

Its food is plankton, the microscopic organisms of the sea on which the great whales feed, though small squids or fish are equally acceptable. But, in mid-winter, the sea and the food it contains can be a hundred miles or more from its rookery site, so the bird has to find a means of storing this food. Its solution is to convert the food it catches to an inch thickness of blubber. This coating of resilient tissue lies between the skin and the flesh, serving not only as a reserve of food but also as additional insulation against the cold. On land it progresses in a dignified walk standing upright on its stumpy legs, but also, when alarmed or when it feels insecure ice or soft snow beneath its feet, it falls on its stomach and toboggans along, pushing itself forward with paddling motions of its powerful flippers. In neither of these forms of progress is the accumulated layer of blubber any great handicap. In movement, thus, it carries several months' food wherever it goes and is capable of surviving in the worst blizzard on land or the heaviest gale at sea. There remains one other problem for the breeding Emperor. The Emperor penguin feeds its chick by regurgitating partly digested plankton which the chick receives by putting its head into the open beak of its parent; but that food has to be brought in the parent's stomach from the sea many weeks' march away. Normally, it would be digested long before the parent returned, so that on arrival the parent would have an empty stomach and nothing to regurgitate for its chick. The solution was found on dissecting the stomach of a returning female Emperor. A membrane, quite abnormal for any bird, was found to have formed in the stomach, sealing off and protecting from normal digestion the ration of plankton destined for the hungry chick.

Biologically and physiologically, the Emperor penguin shows a marvellous adaptation for a difficult and extraordinary form of life. But these defences of the Emperor against the wind and the cold—when the wind can scream at 100 knots with a temperature of −30° C.—are not altogether adequate, so the Emperor has adopted additional techniques to combat really bad weather. With the onset of each blizzard, the birds come together in compact circular groups all facing inward with their backs to the raging elements, thus by mutual protection they arrest the escape of body heat.

We were to know the Emperor penguin well before the year was out, for, although Prévost the biologist was charged with their study, all the rest of the party were at one time or another called in to aid in some phase of the study. But, quite apart from that, with the Emperor the only living thing apart from the men in the area for many long months, it was not surprising that we observed their ways with the sympathy of a fellow animal.

In mid-March we had a glorious day. Not a cloud broke

the azure blue expanse of the sky. There was not a breath of wind. Though the temperature was —10° C., it was quite comfortable wandering about outside in a light jersey. The bay was mirror-like, and the only disturbance on its tranquil, dark blue surface was when, now and then, an Emperor penguin surfaced. At the rookery site, part of the bay had frozen over and the first arrivals were already establishing themselves on this three-inch-thick sheet of ice. A continuous watch was begun at the rookery, which at this time, was still separated from Isle des Pétrels by unfrozen water, although observation was obscured by Ile Rostand between us and the rookery.

For this purpose we had in our stores a small prefabricated hut, a box of plywood six feet square, which we planned to use at the Emperor rookery site to provide a shelter and observation post. Marret decided to take advantage of this unusually fine weather to establish this little hut on Ile Rostand.

A barge was loaded with sections of the hut, food, fuel, a primus stove and sleeping gear for the two men, as well as tools for the erection of the hut and a motor-driven rock drill to drill staples into the rock. These would act as anchors to tie the hut down against the wind. It made a heavy load and it had to be pulled down to the water's edge by the dogs. From the main hut to the water's edge was a steep slope of icy snow and, looking at it from above, there seemed a good chance that, once the dogs got the barge under way and on to the ice slope, the barge would take charge and drag dogs and contents into the water. Accordingly, a system of braking was arranged with crowbars before the dogs were harnessed on. Then 'Ee-ee les chiens!' And away we went.

Marret and I started frantically braking with the crowbars to slow up the barge from taking charge. The dogs, however, looking back, saw the mass of the barge bearing down on them, and strained at their traces to get away from it. As a result, the load gathered speed, getting out of control. I had visions of dogs being run down by the careering mass of the barge, plunging head on into the water and dragging the mangled remains of the team with it to the bottom. But the dogs saw the water ahead of them, and when commanded swung to one side, still straining madly at their harness. When the excitement died down the barge was broadside on to the ice cliff at the water's edge, only ten feet from it.

Marret was inclined to blame me because using the dogs had been my idea, but it was much too beautiful a day for recriminations. We got the barge into the water by unloading it, then reloading it once it was in. An outboard motor was attached to drive it. Jackie Duhamel followed the barge in our little dinghy to pick up survivors in case of an accident.

The water was the purest of sapphire blues and despite the ice and temperatures of the air, was so clear and tranquil that it was an invitation to plunge in. It did not look at all cold, even though a scum of ice crystals were forming on the surface. The smallest fragment of ice floating past was an emerald and diamond cluster of jewels clasped in a setting of clear blue water. Every facet of every ice crystal caught the sunlight and glistened. The blackness of the exposed rocks of the island served as a foil to enhance the crystal white of the snow. The little outboard motor chugged the heavily loaded barge across the bay amid this cold splendour at the magnificent speed of about one knot. Snow and ice in the Antarctic is never flat white, it always reflects the blue of the sky, the green of the water and the reds of a low sun. On that day this world of colour was so accentuated as to be unreal.

It was a disappointment when the barge came to a halt at the miniature ice cliff under Ile Rostand, putting an end to this tranquil absorption of the beauty of the scene. With the barge moored against the land and its nose driven against the thin sheet of newly formed ice leading to the rookery, we commenced the work of unloading.

It was hot work, and before long we had stripped to the waist and were still perspiring. As we unloaded we saw Emperors making their way fussily over the new ice leading to the rookery. They arrived shooting along under water like torpedoes. Then as they approached the edge of the ice they came to the surface at a steep angle at top speed, which brought them flying into the air to land heavily on their stomachs on the ice. They got to their feet, shook the snow off their coats and, after looking about, made their way in Indian file to the rookery. This jumping technique was their normal method of coming from the water on to the floe ice but here there were frequent accidents when the thin new ice broke under the impact of the heavy body. Then the Emperor found he had passed through and was once more in the water. Not the least deterred, he headed seaward again to gain enough distance to pick up the necessary speed; he turned again and rushed the ice edge for a second attempt. One particularly heavy chap had five attempts before he finally made it.

Being prefabricated, the hut took very little time to erect. The biggest task was drilling holes for anchor spikes in the rock. Once this was done, steel wire cables were passed over the roof of the little hut and tied down to steel pins let into the rock and the hut was complete. The sea was showing signs of freezing over as the day progressed; the little frost crystals seen earlier in the day were becoming denser and denser, and a heavy scum of semi-solid ice, known as brash, was forming over the surface of the bay. The heavy barge was sent back to Ile des Pétrels to avoid having it frozen in, the little dinghy being retained to ferry the men back and forth. By the close of the day Jackie Duhamel was having difficulty in rowing the dinghy through the water, for the brash was several inches thick and almost in a solid state. Prévost and Rivolier remained at the little hut to begin the programme of continuous observation of the Emperors, and the rest of us returned to the main hut. Two days later the bay froze over, and Ile des Pétrels ceased to be an island and was once more connected to the mainland. Thereafter traffic between the two points was by means of the dogs and sledge.

Prévost and Rivolier reported that they had found the little hut most uncomfortable. Its thin, uninsulated walls of three-ply gave little protection from the cold and their breath and the vapour from their cooking condensed as ice on the roof and walls. This accumulated rime melted when they ran their primus and water dropped on sleeping-bags and gear, only to freeze again the moment the primus was stopped. During the night the temperature at the roof was —10° C., but at the door it was —20° C. Apparently quite a lot had to be done to make the little box habitable.

We decided to use Pickles' team for transporting men and goods to and from the rookery, since these were all older dogs and were considered safer with penguins than the young ones. In this way we hoped that for a while the young dogs would not be aware that the Emperor penguin rookery existed. From then on, for several weeks, we took turns occupying the hut and observing the Emperors. Each relief was charged in its spare time to work on the little hut in order to make it more habitable. Every time the dog team went to the hut it took any odd scraps of timber and packing-cases that could be found near the camp to act as building materials for the improvement of the hut.

A typical day at this time was when Marret and Vincent were to relieve Lépineux and Rivolier at the little hut. I harnessed up my dogs to the sledge while the two men dug about the snowdrifts for odd ends of packing-cases to take with them. Once these were loaded on the sledge and tied down—for it was a boisterous day with strong wind and medium drift—we all piled aboard the sledge and went racing down the slope to the bay. At the tide crack, where the floating bay ice joins the static land-based ice, was a cliff some six feet high. For a few yards the margin of the floating ice was always smashed into fragments by tide action, leaving a belt of water filled with ice fragments and brash. The dogs did not like this at all, and always balked at the edge. They had an inherent fear of water, for every one of them at one time or another had had the unpleasant experience of falling into the water in such a place. When they finally scrambled out their wet fur froze solid immediately. Now, the only way to get them across was to grab Pickles and throw him over. Nelson and Bobby followed voluntarily, but Aspirin and Pomme hung back at the end of their traces with their feet dug into the ice, resisting all attempts to dislodge them. While the men edged them forward, the other three, Pickles, Bobby and Nelson now on firm ice, were also driven forward. Once the whole team were on the floating ice, the sledge and contents automatically followed in a rush, ending with a crash at the bottom.

The sea ice in this early stage was very difficult for sledging. A layer of salty brash overlay the formed ice and sledge runners pulled heavily through it as though running on liquid glue. So, though the dogs could pull the load and driver, the two passengers had to walk along behind the sledge.

We were surprised to find the Emperor penguin rookery had moved around Ile Rostand, thus being no longer visible from the little observation hut. It seemed inconsiderate of the penguins to wait until we had gone to all the trouble of erecting the hut and modifying it, to find that no sooner was it done than they had shifted their quarters.

Prévost and Lépineux were with the birds, armed with materials for numbering them. Several startled Emperors were wandering about the rookery with large identification numbers in red paint on their backs. While Prévost was explaining to Marret and Vincent what they should do during their tour of duty, I ran on to the hut with the sledge cargo and their packs. An open porch had been built out from the door side with packing-case ends. All the stores of the hut were now stacked in this porch. Further work with canvas had insulated the walls a bit. But it still looked damp and confined within. On one side was a bookcase; a small table served as writing bench and work table. Along the walls were shelves, built high up so that the rising heat of the primus would tend to thaw out the tins of food stored there. A further shelf supported a cylinder of propane gas and a gas burner. A steak of penguin meat had been hanging above the primus to thaw when the morning's cooking was done, but now was frozen stiff as a board. Sleeping-bags were rolled against the wall.

A snarling and a yelping from the dogs outside told me that something was going on that required my attention. The sledge was against the side of the hut and a tangled mass of dogs were quarreling. They had found the box of penguin meat stored outside the hut and most of it had already disappeared. Something told me that Marret and Vincent would be opening a can or two that night.

The packs and sleeping-bags of the last occupants were standing against the door, so I loaded these and went down at a run to the rookery and joined the others. I found them at the edge of the bay ice watching the Emperors arriving, direct from the sea. We would see a head break the surface some twenty yards from the edge of the ice and then a little later there would be an Emperor shooting through the air out of the water to land on the ice with a thump. Sometimes, there would be as many as ten penguins in the air at once. It was rather like watching a magician pull rabbits out of a hat; one moment there would be a bare expanse of ice and the next half a dozen Emperor penguins would have materialized.

Prévost, in the course of his study, had to kill a number of the Emperors for dissection. Though it seemed a crime to kill these beautiful and quaint creatures, not only did the victims serve the purposes of science to the utmost, but the flesh provided the fresh meat that we needed so much. Then what was left, after Prévost and the cook had taken their share, was fed to the dogs to spread out the seal meat reserves. Before leaving he killed three. His first attempts to kill the birds as humanely as possible had not met with a great deal of success; he used chloroform and that required two men to hold the frantically struggling bird and one to administer the anaesthetic. The captive usually defended himself with shrewd blows of his bone-hard flippers and it could be truly said that the anaesthesia of an Emperor penguin hurt the men much more than the penguin. Of late, however, he had developed a much more efficient and humane method. He walked behind the selected victim until close enough and struck it on the back of the neck with the haft of an ice-axe. The victim crumpled up without so much as a quiver.

The dogs watched the whole proceedings with a curiosity which was not altogether disinterested. As each penguin arrived and started to waddle its way to the main group of the rookery five pairs of eyes would follow his every move. Pomme and Aspirin, more so than the others, left no doubt as to what would happen at the Emperor rookery if ever they broke loose and found their way there. Nelson and Bobby, who in the dog lines were always noted for their peculiar conduct—Nelson for his half-witted behaviour and Bobby for his masochism—became more or less normal citizens out with the sledge. The way they were licking their lips and watching the Emperors walking past was perfectly normal husky behaviour.

Very soon we were heading back to camp with three penguin bodies lashed on the sledge and the dogs spread out in their fan traces, pulling their hardest as they always did when homeward bound. The moment the team came into view of the dog lines as it emerged from the bergs frozen in the bay, all the dogs in camp began to howl. A sledge going out or coming in is always a signal for howling by the dogs left behind. This howling about the camp was so much part of our lives that if it had not happened I am sure we would have missed it just as much as if the hut itself had suddenly vanished. Nick, the supposed invalid of Pickles' team, was delighted to see the rest of his team arrive. Because he had a stiffness in his back from a blow with a whip handle during a fight at Port Martin, Nick was spared sledge work to give him the best chance of recovery. However, he always became highly excited when the team left and would be seen leaping against his chain pleading to be taken too.

While I was tying up the team in their places in the dog lines Nick launched an attack on Pickles, the big leader. I expected Nick to be massacred on the spot, as Pickles was a powerful and courageous dog. If Nick's fighting ability was any criterion to his state of health, he was a very well dog indeed. He was a match for Pickles, the leader, or nearly so, for the two big dogs surged backward and forward snapping and snarling in furious combat, and frequently it seemed that the despised Nick was gaining the upper hand. Bobby, usually the victim of Nick's quarrels, fell on his stomach on the ground, covering his nose with his forepaws, his eyes tightly closed, snarling weakly and waiting for the inevitable savaging. When some moments had passed and the expected attack had not materialized, Bobby cautiously opened one eye and saw his enemy fully engaged with Pickles. A gleam of joy lit up his eyes and in a moment he was on his feet, snarling happily as he pranced about the two fighting dogs, at each opportunity giving any exposed por-

tion of Nick a shrewd bite. The chance was too good to miss!
Not once did he attempt to bite Pickles.

Once a dog fight such as this breaks out in the dog lines,
all the other dogs become highly excited, and in next to no
time there is not one dog fight in progress but half a dozen.
Immediately beyond Pickles and Nick, the two big Labradors, Aspirin and Pomme, were struggling together. A little
farther on Bjorn was beating up Fram, on principle, while
Maru leapt madly against his chain screaming with excitement. In Boss's team, Boss himself was snarling at Astro and
Seismo was attacking Wild. Tiki, a confirmed food hoarder,
was at the end of his chain cautiously stealing a piece of
Milk's food while Milk's attention was held by Bjorn and
Fram rolling about next to him. It was a full quarter of an
hour before peace was once more restored among the dogs.
Although most of the combatants were licking wounds, it
was easily seen that all concerned considered it had been a
quarter of an hour well spent. I was just returning to the
sledge to unravel harnesses, feeling that the disturbance
had passed off without any consequence, when I was horrified to see an empty collar on a chain at the end of Bjorn's
team. Maru had broken loose and under cover of the general
excitement had slipped away. Out of the corner of my eye
I saw Maru slinking over the skyline towards the Adelie
penguin rookery behind the camp. Pausing only long enough
to snatch a whip off the sledge I raced off in hot pursuit. By
the time I arrived on the scene the carnage had already
begun. At first I could not see Maru, but a trail of dead and
dying penguins led direct to where he was at work among
the rocks. This was not killing for food but killing for the
sheer lust of killing and the taste of hot blood. He was horribly efficient, a quick sideways bite and another penguin
lay quivering and bleeding. He had barely released it before
his jaws closed down on the next. He saw me arriving and
began to edge away but still paused momentarily in his re-

treat to kill other penguins. The chase finished with me a few yards behind Maru, cutting at him with the whip but with Maru still methodically killing. He could have easily escaped the cuts of the whip by abandoning the slaughter and taking to full flight, but he did not. He quickened his pace enough to keep just ahead of me and steadily continued the killing. In the end he paused just too long over a victim and I was able to slip the whip lash about his neck. I was both exhausted and furious. But, although I beat him unmercifully on the spot, I knew that it served no useful purpose, for when dragging him back to the dog lines, as we passed each group of the surviving Adelies that same longing I knew so well lit up his eyes and his great tongue licked across his bloodstained lips in both memory and anticipation.

Prévost estimated that that ten minute sortie resulted in one hundred and fifty dead Adelie penguins. This was nothing compared to Aspirin's slaughter a year ago at Port Martin; five thousand in one afternoon.

This was not the sole result of the day's disturbance however. Today's fight was to prove the beginning of a marathon battle between the two Labradors, Pomme and Aspirin. Pomme was the son of Aspirin as nearly as one could tell, considering the doubtful pedigree of all the huskies; in any case he was an exact replica in appearance of the old reprobate. Neither of these two had ever won great renown as fighters; slow moving and heavy they were no match for the other swift wolfish dogs, and they themselves were well aware of the fact. However, in each other they both found an antagonist to their liking. Both being heavily haired and short mouthed they were unable to seize anything but a jawful of fur when they snapped. They enjoyed most of the joys of fighting without its more painful consequences. After that first encounter the battle continued for weeks on end, uninterrupted except for breathing spells and sleep. They would stand on their hind legs and worry at each other, like two heavy-weight wrestlers manœuvring. Some days, Aspirin's accumulated wisdom won over Pomme's inexperience, and on other days Pomme's youthful vitality prevailed over Aspirin's age and natural laziness. Aspirin was also handicapped a little in that chained below him was Pickles, who from time to time, excited by their snarling and growling, would break the boredom of the daily round by nipping Aspirin. Pomme, being the last dog on the line of that team, only had to contend with Aspirin.

At this time Bjorn's team was undoubtedly the best. It consisted of Bjorn, the leader and the biggest, strongest and most unintelligent dog we had; Fram, his sycophant of a lieutenant and undoubtedly the most intelligent and laziest; the bitch Ifaut, an intelligent and beautiful creature; Maru, the terror of the penguin rookeries; Milk and Tiki the two inseparables; and Yacka, the young bitch, replacing Helen who had been moved into Boss's team.

Maru and Yacka were close friends. Being chained together and both being young dogs, they were soon playing together. Each day they would manage to twist and knot their chains together until they finished with their two collars side by side incapable of movement until someone took pity on them and unravelled the two chains. However Maru was not a gentleman. He quite unashamedly stole Yacka's food and bullied her unmercifully, but for all that Yacka seemed to like this cave-dog treatment and fawned over him.

Since Bjorn's team was the best available, it was the one most in demand for odd work with the dog sledge. However, for short trips about the bay or across to the Emperor penguin rookery, we rarely used the full team but harnessed up just Maru, Fram and Bjorn. If any weight was to be pulled the team was strengthened by the addition of Milk and Tiki or the two bitches.

At that time I was doing a little survey work about the immediate vicinity. A typical day was when I went to the

Carrel to read a few theodolite angles, taking the dog sledge drawn by Bjorn, Fram, Maru, Milk and Tiki. Naturally enough, on the empty sledge I went away at a flat run. But the empty sledge with five dogs is very difficult to stop, in fact impossible if the dogs do not co-operate. Another difficulty is that the dogs remember routes previously used, and at each departure assume that the objective is the place visited on the last run out, so head direct for that. Once the creatures have such an idea firmly implanted in their minds it takes a lot of effort and swearing to take them anywhere else.

In this case the last trip out had been to the Emperor rookery and I could sense as we careened down the ice slope from the hut that that was where they had decided we were heading this time. However, the team pulled up just before the tide crack, eyeing it suspiciously, especially Bjorn. He very cautiously approached the drop down to the sea ice in response to my urging, but the moment he saw the brash between landfast and floating ice he came backing away rapidly. The rest of the team remained at the edge peering over doubtfully. Maru, in response to urging from behind, launched himself into space and landed heavily among the broken ice, managing to scramble through the brash to firm floating ice. I would like to credit Maru with courage for this action but could not help feeling that Fram might have had something to do with his sudden leap. For Fram, that most intelligent dog, once he saw that nothing really drastic had happened to Maru, immediately followed suit. Then Milk and Tiki jumped leaving me with all the team across the tide crack except the leader, Bjorn, who had backed away as far as his trace would permit him and was whining his objections to the whole procedure like the great oaf that he was.

'Sometimes, Bjorn,' I told him, 'I'm ashamed of you. Don't you realize that the main duty of a leader is to lead?'

Bjorn did not see it that way at all, so the only way I could get him over was to drive the rest of the team ahead dragging Bjorn, still protesting and resisting, with the sledge across the crack. However, once safely across, Bjorn immediately considered the incident closed and became his normal aggressive and annoying self, barging to the front, pausing for a moment to bully Fram and Maru, then heading towards the Emperor rookery instead of in the right direction in which the rest had already been heading.

'Yuck, Bjorn, yuck les chiens,' I called, giving the order to swing left. I could see poor Bjorn's overtaxed brain wrestling with the problem. Finally making up his mind, he looked back with an air of relief at having made an important decision and then headed off to the right. Fram and the others, acting on the command, began to swing left, but, seeing Bjorn head right, swung round to follow him. It was impossible ever to become really annoyed with Bjorn, he always meant so well and tried so hard.

I left the sledge turned over (to prevent the dogs from running away with it) and the five dogs grouped around it to climb up to the top of the island with the theodolite, and commenced my work. From there I could look down on the dogs to see what mischief they were brewing. Apart from Bjorn's usual bullying of the others, and especially of Fram, their behaviour was exemplary, no doubt to lure me into a false sense of security for the villainies to follow. The temperature was quite low and there was a little sharp wind coming away from the south that kept frostbiting my face and gradually chilling my hands as I worked on the theodolite.

It was a pleasure to turn away from the breeze to face the weak sun. From time to time I was obliged to stop work to run round the rocks to restore circulation. By the time I had finished my observations my main interest was to rejoin the dogs and head back to the warm hut by the shortest route.

When I got down to the sledge, Bjorn was on his feet to greet me by pushing his head between my legs, a habit of his, with his back arched for a rub along his spine

I righted the sledge, strapped on my gear, and in doing so took off a glove to knot the tie rope. The glove slipped and blew away a few yards. I turned to get it, then the dogs were away like the wind. I made a frantic grab at the steering handle, but only succeeded in falling face downwards on the hard ice. Meanwhile the five scoundrels shot away at top speed with the sledge banging along behind them.

To my horror I suddenly realized they were heading in the direction of the Emperor penguin rookery. 'Whoa!' was quite useless; they had not the least interest in stopping; they had their liberty and intended to make the best possible use of it. My only chance was to attempt to turn them in a less dangerous direction.

'*Heely! Heely!*' I called, giving the order for a turn to the right, and to my infinite relief they swung round and headed up the island on a steep ice slope to disappear over the crest out of sight. At least mass murder had been averted.

When I finally caught them, I found they had dragged the sledge into a mass of broken boulders, a proceeding not calculated to do the sledge a great deal of good, and had only halted because the sledge had jammed between the rocks and stopped them. Otherwise they would probably have been still running. They were lying about looking very pleased and rather expecting a reward for their cleverness. They got a reward of a sort.

Driving them back down the ice slope was a tricky business, and they headed off at a rate of knots with me vainly braking with both feet to stop the mad downhill rush. On a piece of rough ice the sledge bounced high in the air and, once more, I took leave of the sledge to leave the dogs free to career on without me. This time however Bjorn saw the tide crack at the edge of the island and veered away to the

left. Following the high ice on the island side of the tide
track they went racing off round the island.

As I came panting round a rock corner I found them
stopped again. This time the sight that met my eyes was the
five dogs sitting on the edge of the miniature ice cliff and the
sledge dangling over at the end of their harness. The dogs
were too scared to be helpful and the sledge was too awk-
ward for me alone to drag back over the edge of the little
cliff. The only way I could resolve the problem was to lower
the dogs individually on their traces after the sledge, dropping them into the brash beneath. In overcoming their resistance, I nearly followed the sledge. But the experience
seemed to sober the miscreants. Each one scrambled on to a
large piece of ice in the brash at the base of the ice cliff and
stoically awaited my arrival. Bjorn was so miserable that by
the time I had the five of them and the sledge on sound floating ice he even forgot to blame Fram for their misfortunes.
It was a very sad and sorry group that headed back to the
hut.

Before turning in that night I moved Ifaut from the dog
lines to a kennel in the maternity hospital. I was pleased to
note during the night that she was not a non-stop howler
like Helen.

However, Bjorn added to the nightly noise on finding his
mate had been removed from the lines.

4

Preliminary Skirmishing

Ifaut's pups were four beauties and Ifaut proved to be an ideal mother. While Judy had found it difficult to protect just Paton from the cold and wind, and Helen had not even tried, the gentle Ifaut made the kennel a warm little haven for the four little bundles of fur nestled in against her stomach.

We called the puppies Matthew, Sandra, Janet and Bora. Matthew was a little replica of Maru; Ifaut herself was mirrored in Janet; there was something reminiscent of Yacka in Sandra, while Bora, the biggest of the four, bore a striking resemblance to Bjorn. So it always was with these dogs; always, from long inbreeding, the old types reappeared.

Paton, who now was capable of wandering short distances from Judy, was beginning to venture a little farther afield. Judy did not like it at all, and the moment that Paton's plump little body got out of reach of her chain and her protection, she screamed with anxiety until one of the men brought the little adventurer back to her. Judy knew her own kind, and was fully aware of what would happen to an appetizing morsel like Paton if he arrived alone near one of the grown dogs. However, one day Paton noticed Ifaut and the pups outside their case taking advantage of a rare period of fine weather and the weak warmth of the low autumn sun. I, fortunately, as it happened, was watching. Paton was still very plump, by virtue of being an only pup, so he had difficulty in making his way over the short distance between him and the pups. Ifaut was too busy licking over one of her own to notice the intruder at once. With any other dog but the gentle Ifaut I would have been more cautious about allowing Paton to approach so close.

Paton was saved only because Ifaut's own pups yelped as she sprang. The yelp of the pups as they were flung aside was just enough to make her misjudge her slashing bite, and Paton, instead of being laid open, was thrown several yards. Ifaut stood with her head low and her teeth bared in the wolf snarl of the husky. The transformation of the gentle Ifaut I thought I knew so well to this murderous beast was a shock.

Bjorn's team did not seem the same in Ifaut's absence. There was a lack of cohesion in their work. The bitch of the team is the nucleus about which the team is built. The relationship of leader and bitch is always a near man and wife arrangement. Bjorn never showed the least interest in any other bitch and Ifaut showed no inclination for any dog but Bjorn.

Whenever Bjorn was hitched in his traces—as leader he was harnessed first—and I was away getting the next dog in the team, there would be a scurry, and the sledge would be bounding across the rocks, and I would find Bjorn licking noses with Ifaut at the maternity hospital. Ifaut, too, always seemed glad to see him but took the precaution of bundling her little ones into the case before he arrived.

We decided to break in Yacka, Roald's playmate, to sledge work. Yacka was the most unlike a sledge dog of all the dogs. She was much more a collie than anything else, being long haired, long snouted and fine in build. It seemed strange that such a strain could have cropped up in the Labradors and Greenlanders. However, she was a bitch, and whether she could pull or not, at least she could fill the place of Ifaut in the team for a little while.

The first day I took her out in harness was disheartening. A husky pulls steadily, one leg after the other, with his body low to the ground and his legs widespread to give the maximum of purchase. Yacka pulled in hops, leaping against her harness, slackening and leaping again. Being so young she could not concentrate on pulling like the others, but was constantly stopping to look at objects that attracted her attention. Then, finding herself behind the rest of the team, she would race off in her hopping manner after them and, in doing so, tangle herself among the harness ropes of the others. The dogs did not seem to consider her a satisfactory replacement for Ifaut. But as Ifaut would be some months with her pups, we had to fill up the teams somehow, and Yacka and Pomme were all we had as replacements.

We planned a trip in order to test the serviceability of our gear, especially certain innovations, and also to familiarize the men with the gear and with the dogs. Two teams of seven dogs were to be used, and there were two men to each sledge. Marret and Rivolier took Bjorn's team while Duhamel and I took the young dogs under grizzled old leader Boss, this latter team being only half trained compared with Bjorn's.

Duhamel and I led away. Wise old Boss, having once been set off in the right direction, needed no further commands. Whereas any other dog we owned was incapable of maintaining a given direction for any length of time, old Boss, with his many years of experience in sledging, ran direct for the objective. The cut of the sledge runners behind was straight without the slightest deviation.

Away behind us was the second team, a barely visible black dot on the sea ice plain. They had been delayed, so we had a lead of half an hour on them. Each sledge was self-supporting; it carried its own camp gear, food for both dogs and men, as well as a tent. The load was heavy and bulky.

The point selected for the trial camp was a nunatak on the coast, an outcrop of black rocks. It was pleasant on the sea ice that day; the temperatures were moderate and there was only the lightest of winds. There was little snow lying on the ice surface, so the sledge ran easily and effortlessly while the dogs pulled with their tails high in the air, their faces coated in rime from their moisture-laden breaths.

We were soon at a halt on a section of level, wind-swept ice against the rocks of the nunatak. We wasted no time in staking out the dog chains and attaching our dogs. Once the dogs were fed, the tent was erected, our gear bundled inside, and a warm mug of pemmican hoosh was set to bubbling over the primus. A little later Marret and Rivolier were with us, and pitched their tent a little away from our own.

Duhamel and I were quite comfortable in our pyramid tent but Marret and Rivolier in their little Alpine tent were not so happy. The temperature was —27° C. and there was a strong wind carrying medium drift snow. The accumulated drift about their tent squeezed the walls and the rime condensed from their breathing lay nearly an inch thick on the inner walls. When they lit their primus the rime melted momentarily, dripped, and formed ice. Their tent was fast becoming untenable. So we turned our backs on the plateau and broke camp for a return to base.

Descending the big drift down from the land ice to the bay, my sledge slipped sideways on the steep bank and, in a moment went tumbling down to finish on its back. While I was repacking it, Rivolier driving the second one came hurtling out of space with his team and sledge and, before anything could be done, the two teams were engaged in a glorious free for all. This was a major catastrophe when dog-driving; fourteen dogs each on a separate trace mixed up in a general brawl, tangling their own and every harness into a Gordian knot. Of course the dogs love it. While I and Rivolier would be busy disentangling one pair of furious but happy fighters, the rest would be doing their best to spread further confusion.

Helen, the little black beast, was in her element. She never seemed so happy as when blood and fur was flying in a normal brawl, but here where even the unwilling dogs were obliged to join in because their tangled traces prevented their escape, she was delirious with joy.

Fram rather surprised me. Normally overshadowed by Bjorn's bullying and forceful character, this time he found himself on the other side of the melee from Bjorn and, instead of cringing and fawning as he usually did, was well in the brawling, aggressively savaging every dog that he could reach.

Maru, the penguin-killing philosopher, crawled to a point of safety alongside the sledge and, unnoticed by all, quietly got to work on a food bag.

Poor Pomme, the big Labrador cross, would have liked to do the same but never got a chance, finding himself in the exact centre of the seething mass of snapping dogs. Old Boss backed against the sledge, where he could meet all his enemies head on, and gave a good account of himself with his jaws and muzzle smeared with blood.

When it was finally sorted out, no dog was seriously hurt, all were looking fully satisfied with the proceedings, and in licking wounds reminiscently, considered the whole thing a most enjoyable respite from the serious business of sledging.

We were only in camp for that one night. The following day found the teams heading northward with the object of establishing a camp at the most northerly island and from there making a quick run farther to the north in the hope of discovering how far the Emperor penguins had to go before they found open water in which to feed. I was once more driving Boss's team, led by the old warrior himself, while

Prévost drove Bjorn's. Georges Lépineux made the third member of the party.

It was becoming noticeable that Boss was beginning to fail, that the lower temperatures of approaching winter were chilling his old frame. From time to time the trace that normally was as tight as a violin string, and which, I am sure, was a point of pride to the indomitable old dog, fell slack. A flick of the driving whip would tighten up his trace but only momentarily. The trouble was not unwillingness but sheer age and lost stamina; his gallant spirit spurred him on and he was willing to pull in his harness until he died, but the blood no longer flowed so freely to warm him in the bitter cold, and the once resilient and tireless muscles had stiffened with age. He well merited a quiet corner by the fire after a lifetime of toil, but instead he was still leading his team in the drifting snow and bitter cold.

We camped on the windswept sea ice that night at the corner of Ile du Dépot. The ice, warmed by the unfrozen sea water beneath, was much less cold than the land ice of previous camps, where the air temperature had been −25° C. The men were well off, but the dogs were miserable. Since there was little snow lying, they remained exposed to the wind and did not become buried in the snow as usually happened.

Each dog grabbed his rock-like ration of frozen seal meat and, snarling, began to gnaw away at it, watching each of his neighbours jealously lest they steal it. Not much of a life, this late autumn sledging. Pulling a sledge all day with the wind cutting and cold, the fine drift snow packing into fur and forming ice, and a rim of hard-frozen breath condensed about the muzzle, yet with the driver calling him to keep moving every time a dog halted to bite away a little of the ice that had accumulated. Then at the close of the day being staked out where the sledge halted for the night, no cover, the only protection from the wind the snow that the wind carries burying him slowly, and the highlight of the day a two-pound piece of seal meat that is frozen so hard that an axe bounces off it, striking sparks, and that has to be gnawed and licked to thaw it.

Veritably a dog's life!

It was not much fun getting away the next morning. Although we had no thermometer with us it was easy to tell that the temperature had fallen considerably. The dogs were dancing from one foot to the other to avoid contact with the cold snow. Prévost's ginger beard was snow white from his breath that was condensing on it, and icicles were forming off our faces. Wrestling with dog harnesses and particularly with their clips of metal which called for bare hands was difficult and we were all glad, dogs included, to be under way when the body heat liberated by movement helped to battle against the cold.

We ran away to the northward with light sledges and left the pitched tent behind us at Ile du Dépot, intending to make as much northing as we could in following the tracks of the feeding Emperors, and to return to the tent the same day.

Even with the lightened sledges it was heavy going, for the surface was irregular and covered with a deep layer of wind-cut snow, like the waves of a frozen, choppy sea. Boss was magnificent, it was hard to believe that he was not a one-year-old like the rest of his swift-stepping team. Seismo, the little tough, made a nuisance of himself all day being in a more aggressive mood than usual. At each opportunity he launched an attack on one of the other dogs. But although he was unafraid of any other dog in the team he was completely under Boss's sway, and a growl from the old leader would send Seismo recoiling in terror.

Ahead of me was Prévost and Lépineux driving Bjorn's team. Apparently Fram was giving them more than usual trouble with his laziness. Across the few hundred yards of frosty air I could hear the crack of the whip and their calls.

'*Yuck*, Bjorn, *yuck!*' ('Left, Bjorn, left!')

'*Ee* Fram! *Ee* Fram!' ('Get up, Fram, up, Fram.')

'*Ee-ee, les chiens, ee Fram!*' ('Gee up the dogs, up Fram!')

'Fram! *Ee* Fram!'

'*Heely* Bjorn. *Heely* Milk, *ee* Tiki, *ee* Fram!'

And occasionally their sledge would halt, as one of them went forward to punish Fram for his laziness, or Bjorn for bullying the others.

Above the sledge ahead was a little cloud of frost smoke from the floating crystals of the frozen breath of men and dogs. None of us had any wish to ride on our sledges, it was much more comfortable walking or running alongside. It was midday but the sun stood only five degrees above the horizon, showing reddish as at setting, while the wind blew steadily, swirling the drift snow about us continually. Looking back, the continental slope was furry with blizzard and falling away on our right was the long projecting tongue of the Terra Nova Glacier, like a great white wall.

It was hard to realize that the apparently solid surface beneath us was a mere skin of ice about a yard thick over a thousand fathoms of dark cold water, until now and then we would encounter a place where the movement of the floating ice kept a narrow line of unfrozen water showing a deep black against the whiteness of the ice. This is called a lead. The dogs hated the leads and balked when we came to one of them. Only the whip in the hands of the driver would send them across. I think they all knew by instinct what happens to the dog that falls into open water at that time of year. He scrambles out, but before he has time to shake himself the sea water freezes solid in his fur and he becomes a statue of a dog encased in ice.

Bjorn, as usual, was more cowardly than the rest in this respect. I could see the sledge ahead halting at the leads, and frequently at places that Bjorn thought were leads, where the men had to force him to cross. Maru, the philosophic penguin-killer, was a great help to them. He travelled with his nose to the tracks hoping for the best. When the rest of the team halted at a lead Maru went on alone, not letting anything so unimportant as a little water prevent him from closing the distance between himself and the delectable animals that had made those tracks. Once Maru had crossed, the others followed. Perhaps it was Maru's usefuless in this penguin chase that accounted for his later and otherwise inexplicable popularity with Prévost.

My team was not so difficult. Boss, being old and experienced, apart from testing each lead warily, crossed without much need of encouragement. The rest of the team, young and high spirited, followed readily, their interest centred on the team ahead, hoping to catch up with them and break the monotony of the day in a glorious fight. That is why the driver of the following team never has a great deal of trouble. His dogs have always this overpowering urge to catch up with the team ahead. Though experience has taught them that the moment they draw close enough for this to happen their driver will brake the sledge and defeat their hopes, they continue to chase the waving tails ahead.

The dogs were uneasy, for all their bloodthirsty hopes. I do not think they were capable of reasoning out the dangers connected with travelling away from land on the uncertain medium of the sea ice, with each mile leaving another lead between them and the solid land-based ice, and the plateau behind fuzzy with an impending blow, but they seemed to sense instinctively that this apparently firm surface of snow and ice was unsure. Or, perhaps, they sensed the thoughts of the men that were driving them. In any case they were nervous as the miles between them and land dropped astern.

From time to time, we overtook little groups of Emperor penguins heading steadily northward to their distant goal—

the open sea. We timed one little group. Two and a half miles in one hour they made, waddling on in their inevitable single file formation, never hurried, but always moving forward slowly and inevitably to where the frost smoke rose like fog from open water, many, many miles away in the distant north. That was our goal too, we hoped, but as the hours of our available time ran out we realized that it lay beyond our reach; for though the Emperors were amphibious and could survive the break-up of the sea ice under the fury of a blizzard, we and the dogs were not. Prévost was also interested in the big penguins as individuals, for he had marked many of them at the rookery and hoped to find some of the marked penguins amid the little groups. This was not easy to do, mainly because of the dogs. One couldn't blame the dogs for being a little hard to handle when they were held at a halt to watch Prévost running after a group of penguins endeavouring to examine them one by one.

During one of these stops we made an interesting find. Two of the Emperors shuffling clumsily along were found to be carrying eggs. Unlike the others who when chased fell on their stomachs and made off tobboganing with feet and flippers at top speed, these two barely increased their pace for fear of dropping their precious burdens. No doubt these two had waited at the rookery while their mates were away feeding in the north. Gradually they had consumed all their stored food reserves and their pangs of hunger became too much so they left the rookery, impelled by hunger, and headed towards the north and food. They did not desert their charges but clumsily carried their precious eggs with them on the weary march.

We halted our northward march in the lee of a great iceberg caught and held in that frozen sea. Despite the cold and the frost rime condensed all about their heads and chests, the dogs flopped into the snow and gulped mouthfuls of dry cold snow. While I set up a theodolite to fix our position from the stars, Prévost and Lépineux broke open a ration and munched at a handful of biscuits and a block of chocolate. It was cold work on the theodolite for the temperature was low. My breath froze on the cold metal and my eyelashes froze to the eyepiece the moment they touched it.

How infinitely more pleasant was travelling than even a momentary halt, and how quickly the cold worked through our heavy clothing to chill and numb the hands and feet, then creep from the extremities to the body itself. Ten minutes spent unshipping a theodolite, making an observation, then strapping up the sledge load again was more than enough to render hands useless and make feet feel like blocks of ice. Already the dogs were on their feet, lifting and shaking each foot in turn to ease the contact of bare pads on the cruelly cold snow. They too were anxious to be on their way.

It was quite dark as we headed back towards the relative comfort of the little red tent pitched by Ile du Dépot. With no landmarks visible we steered on the stars, in this case the friendly red planet Mars showing clearly to the east. The blizzard we had seen brewing on the plateau was close upon us, and the wind was rising. We drove the dogs as hard as possible to get back to the tent before the blizzard caught us out on the vast plain of the frozen sea.

As we rounded the edge of a berg we saw a dark object ahead in the drift and darkness; not the tent, which was too small to see, but the island with its black rocks showing through the icy gloom. A little later the sledges were drawn up at the tent and the dogs staked out for the night, each jealously gnawing at his piece of frozen seal meat, while in the tent we three, half in our sleeping-bags, were grouped round the primus waiting for a share of the pemmican hoosh warming over it. Nothing tastes so good as pemmican at the end of a hard day.

We were back none too soon, for outside the wind began to howl, the drift to sweep by and the tent vibrated with the rising wind. It would have been a cold, bitter camp and an uncertain one away to the north, had we been caught out on the sea ice.

It was still blowing the next morning with moderate drift as we broke camp in a chilly dawn for the last run of the trip back to the base. It was not so bad for the men, with their heads high above the ground and mostly clear of the drift, but the dogs did not like heading into the driving snow at all. They unconsciously kept swinging off course to get their backs to the wind to avoid the merciless sting of the fine particles of driven snow on their faces. Old Boss dropped back from his usual leading position into the closely bunched team sheltering himself from the wind behind them. I left him there. I considered he had earned a respite after his sterling work of the day and night before.

Camp was at the hut that night, and after seeing our teams back in their places in the dog lines we luxuriated in the warmth of the hut and our bunks.

Ifaut's puppies, Matthew, Sandra, Janet and Bora, were now living in the supply shelter. Ifaut could no longer feed them and their new sharp little teeth had been injuring her. She was back with her team while the four pups gambolled in the comparative warmth of the shelter, being frequently visited by Paton, Judy's pup now half grown, who liked to play with them. When the blizzard sprang up the night before, Vincent was horrified to find Janet and Bora missing and gave the alarm. A search party was organized, for the two pups were hardly capable of surviving outside under such conditions. For half an hour the men prodded among the snowdrifts, and searched in the swirling snow for the missing pups. They had almost given up, for the search under these conditions was almost hopeless, when Paton, who up to this time had been lying under the table of the hut where he always sheltered when conditions outside were inclement, came wandering out to see what all the fuss was about. He seemed to understand as soon as he had poked his nose in the shelter and, after attracting Vincent's attention, headed up towards the 'met' screen. Here he began digging furiously into a newly formed drift and a little later unearthed the end of a little frozen tail which, when followed, led to one of the two missing puppies. They were huddled together shuddering with cold and emitting plaintive little cries from cold and fear but otherwise in no danger that the warmth of the hut would not cure.

This was the beginning of a spell of bad luck for the pups. Judy, Paton's mother, who was now back with her team, was ailing, losing weight and fur and had we left her out in the dog lines exposed she would certainly have died. We had only the shelter for the dogs who were sick, but at present the four pups were in occupation. We carefully checked Judy's reaction to the pups, knowing full well the brutal nature of these dogs especially towards anything weak and helpless. The pups gambolled all over Judy nipping her and sniffing at her while Judy just lay quietly indifferent to them. If she showed any interest it was of a friendly nature. After watching the five of them for half an hour we decided that Judy was safe enough and left them alone in the garage. Half an hour later we found Judy alone in the centre of the garage but no sign of the four little pups. But since she was lying quietly we concluded that the pups had wriggled into hiding among the gear stacked along the sides of the garage as they had the habit of doing. So they had, three of them. As I pulled them out they were shuddering with fear and screamed with terror at the sight of Judy. When Judy moved we saw the reason for their fear. A poor, crushed, pathetic, little mangled body that had been Matthew, was lying half eaten beneath her.

A new place was found for Judy and life resumed its normal routine for the pups. But they showed a marked dislike for the shelter and escaped at any opportunity to the snow outside. Paton being older, was quite free and at liberty to sleep where he wished. He usually preferred to sleep on the lee side of the hut if the weather was normal, but if a bad blow blew up he would be waiting at the door of the hut, and the moment the door was opened would slip in to find a more comfortable billet under the hut table. The moment the wind dropped and the drift died down outside, Paton would be found waiting for someone to open the door and let him out again.

In our absence the non-stop hundred-round battle between the two big Labrador crosses, Pomme and Aspirin, had continued and had now taken a sinister turn; gradually the younger and stronger Pomme had began to assert his his supremacy so that we found old Aspirin cowed and broken-spirited with Pomme bullying him unmercifully. A dog with its spirit broken, as Aspirin's was, is a piteable creature, for all his conscious moments are filled with unreasoning terror, not only of the original aggressor, but of all other dogs. He ceases to eat because his food is stolen by his neighbour, his digestion suffers because he gulps what food he has too quickly lest it be stolen, and he no longer cares for himself but lies down with his attention riveted on his bullying neighbours. So he loses condition and, if not cared for, will certainly die.

To bring Aspirin back to his normal, clumsy, good-natured self he was moved from the dog lines and established in a kennel behind the huts, all alone.

Pomme in his turn was due for a change of team. He was at the time in Pickles' team of six-year-olds but, as a vacancy existed in Boss's team of one-year-olds, he was moved to that team which was of his own age group. Following his victory over Aspirin, Pomme was feeling a little above himself and behaving in a most aggressive manner. I felt that there was a rude shock awaiting the young bully when he struck the young toughs of Boss's team and discovered that not all dogs were so easily terrorized as poor old bumbling Aspirin. He was due to discover painfully that some of them had teeth that were not worn to stumps from years of gnawing at frozen seal meat as were Aspirin's.

To make the discovery as painless as possible he was attached next to Boss. Immediately he had taken stock of the situation he decided to appropriate a piece of meat belonging to the old veteran as he had been in the habit of doing with Aspirin. He was young and strong, but his grappling and wrestling tactics, in which weight and strength had played so great a part with Aspirin, were just clumsy fumbling against the battle-scarred Boss. The brief encounter that followed was like a bludgeon against a rapier.

Aspirin found his new surroundings extremely to his liking. A comfortable kennel close to the hut door, and a steady supply of kitchen refuse as a supplement to his normal diet of seal meat, made life a very pleasant thing. Rather like a country gentleman the old ungainly dog set out to laze his days in comfort far from the madding crowd. As he was never seriously considered as a member of a sledging team, this new status and these new privileges, which at the beginning had been intended as a purely temporary arrangement to enable him to regain his lost spirit and health, grew to be permanent. Once he had recovered no one thought to put him back with his team for we had grown to accept him as part of the scenery. He gave no trouble and showed no desire for a more active life. The only time he ever betrayed any excitement was when he saw me descend to the seal meat depot on feeding days and begin hacking up seal meat for the teams. As my usual feeding route went from the working teams to the pups, and lastly to Aspirin, he would become more and more excited, howling in his deep-throated way and leaping against his chain, all this to make sure that he was not forgotten.

The camp was astir for another journey. Inside the hut we were busy weighing out food and packing it in cloth bags to provide sledging rations for another trip. Outside Vincent worked steadily on our one weasel, getting it in first-class running order for the coming journey, for the stillness of the white spaces was to be broken not by the crack of whips and the howling of dogs but by the roar of the weasel's engine. The journey was again to be in search of the open sea where the Emperor penguins feed. For this the weasel had a distinct advantage over the dogs, for a machine knows no fatigue and can run non-stop for as long as the driver can keep awake, whereas the best of dogs can only run so far each day and must be rested at the end of the day to be ready for the next. The sea ice is no certain medium. It can rest, for weeks and months, a continuous unbroken sheet to the horizon. Then there is a severe gale, and the open sea laps against the shores of the continent, and all the ice is gone taking with it anything on its surface out into the stormy wastes of the southern ocean and into oblivion. For this reason, when one has to travel on it, one travels as quickly as possible limiting the time far from land to the bare minimum. Here lay the great advantage of the weasel; for given good surface it can cover a hundred miles in twenty-four hours, against the twenty to thirty miles of the dog teams.

One night Vincent entered the hut. On his head was an improvised fez. He salaamed in the manner of an Arab to Marret.

'Caiad,' he announced, 'the camel is ready to depart.'

With Vincent's camel, the weasel, went Marret, Vincent and Prévost. I stood on the hill at Ile des Pétrels and watched the weasel ploughing its way northward through soft sastrugied snow (Wavelike ridges formed by the action of the wind on a smooth surface and with their axes at right angles to the wind.) lying on the sea ice, until it had faded to an indistinct dot on the northern horizon.

The hut seemed very empty with only the four of us. Part of our world had gone northward with the weasel. We occupied ourselves with the routine work about the hut but our interests were with our three comrades on the sea ice. Their first radio report gave their position as being twenty miles north with further progress blocked by a field of shattered and hummocky ice in which the weasel could make no progress. They were turning westward in an endeavour to work around the obstacle.

The following day was deathly calm and very cold. Outside the hut we could hear a series of cracks like pistol shots. It was the ice sheet over the rocks contracting in the cold and snapping. Our breath hung in the air in a delicate cloud of glistening ice crystals. With no wind we could walk about comfortably in our jerseys but the cold nipped any exposed flesh. The normally invisible perspiration of our bodies condensed on the outside of our jerseys in a tracery of frost rime. The dogs were uncomfortable, they could be seen ceaselessly lifting one paw after the other to keep their pads from contact with the cold ice. We could not have wished for more perfect weather conditions than this for our comrades in the weasel probing away from land. Under such fair skies they had nothing to fear. But the Antarctic is a fickle jade, she smiles so fair when, at that very moment, a tempest is stirring beneath the placid exterior.

By radio that night their signal came crackling in. They had failed to pierce the barrier of hummocks and continued westward. They were camped for the night at Pointe Eba on good solid ice. To turn their venture to some success they planned on the morrow to make a quick run westward and investigate the coastline beyond Cap Pépin.

We settled down to a quiet night.

We woke to hear the wind screaming in fury. The hut

quivered with each gust. The dutyman went out to read the meteorological instruments. He plunged out of the door into a blinding whirl of wind-driven snow so thick that he disappeared from sight in two paces. A little later he came back and stood in the porch trying to clear the ice and snow from his windproofs. We, who had stayed inside, helped for he could see little through the mask of ice that had formed over his face. It was a warm blizzard with the temperature high and the snow so close to melting point that it was wet and stuck to his clothing.

In the last hour the temperature had risen twenty-five degrees. In the hut we were safe and comfortable. But what of our three comrades camped ten miles from land on the sea ice?

We could picture the scene there. They would be held where they had camped. Movement under such conditions would be impossible. They would have swung the weasel round to head into the wind in order to lessen the wind force on the thin plywood walls of its cabin. Even so the three-ton vehicle would be bucking under the furious onslaught of the wind. With such thick drift the machine would be being buried, so each hour they would be obliged to start the motor and drive forward a few yards to free the tracks. They would be seriously worried as to whether the sea ice was still holding and attached to land, or whether it had already begun to crack and break up into ice floes that the wind was urging away from land out into the wastes of the stormy southern ocean. In a blizzard as thick as this they would know nothing. You could not see a hand held a foot away from your face. The shrieking of the wind would drown all other sounds.

If the ice broke up what would be the first warning they would have? A sickening lurch as the weasel slid sideways off a broken floe, a rush of water into the cabin? Or would they, as they drove forward the next time into the blinding whiteness to clear the tracks, just drive off the edge of their flow into the wind-whipped sea?

For us, in a warm, comfortable hut built on solid rock, it was hard to realize that a few miles away our three comrades were in danger of a particularly cold and unpleasant end. But each time the hut shook with a gust more vicious than usual our thoughts would go to them.

We did not worry about the dogs. This sort of thick blizzard was nothing to them. They merely curl up with their backs to the wind and in next to no time are completely buried and each snug in his blanket of snow, in as close to perfect comfort as a husky can know in this cruel land.

We did not go outside unless we had to; we brought too much snow back into the hut in re-entering. But there was one unavoidable sortie and that was to change the record of the tide gauge which was established in a small shelter some four hundred yards below the hut out on the ice of the bay.

Lépineux and Rivolier left the hut together to carry out this duty but were only gone about ten minutes before they returned with their faces masked in ice and their garments packed with ice and snow. They had managed to struggle about a hundred yards before losing all sense of direction in the driving snow and had only regained the hut with difficulty. We waited an hour until conditions seemed to have eased a little then Lépineux and I tried to carry out the task.

Once out of the shelter of the hut it was like trying to fight a palpable adversary to struggle against the buffeting wind and the sheeting snow. We could lean at an angle of forty-five degrees to the ground on the wind and yet still be blown off our feet backwards in the gusts. Visibility was nil. I could not see my own feet. After five yards we could no longer see the hut. All we could see was swirling snow. We were guided by nothing more than the feel of the surface underfoot and the memory of the slope down to the bay as it was in fine weather. The ice forming on our faces, about our wrists, and wherever it could find a chink in the armour of our windproofs hurt like a burn from an iron. We found and recognized the tide crack, where the floating bay ice meets the land ice, by falling into it. Having found this we struck out in the direction of the tide gauge shelter, pacing out of the distance as we went.

At the estimated position of the tide gauge shelter we stopped. I circled about while Lépineux stood still to preserve a sense of direction. We had missed it. The only thing to do was to return to the tide crack and strike out afresh. In a blizzard one soon loses all sense of direction and, worse still, the ability to think logically. This second time we lost count of our paces and it was only after what seemed an interminable period of groping and stumbling that we found ourselves floundering in the broken ice of a tide crack. Something was wrong. Perhaps we had turned in a half circle and were back in the tide crack under the hut or perhaps we had struck the tide crack about one of the other islands in the bay. Communication by voice in this hostile wind was almost impossible but we managed by putting our ice-crusted faces together to exchange ideas.

We decided we must have blundered into the tide crack at Ile Rostand, so turned and headed back in what we hoped was the direction of the hut. Having made this decision, the only thing to do was to act upon it until it proved hopelessly wrong. All the same it was an uncomfortable sensation groping forward blindly in the intense drift, battling against the cruel wind, trying to break the ice masks formed on our faces sufficiently to see a little in momentary easings of the sheeting snow. And wondering whether our slow deliberate progress was taking us towards the warm hut or out northward into the unknown.

Suddenly about a yard in front of my nose I thought I saw a dark object loom and disappear. I stopped a minute, trying to peer into the white murk to decide whether I had really seen something or not. Deciding it was just imagination I took a step forward and collided with a hard vertical wall.

Fumbling round it I identified it as the wall of the elusive tide gauge. It was a very pleasant thing to feel the solid wood and to have this concrete evidence that we were no longer wandering lost about the bay.

There was only room for one in the shelter, so while Lépineux wriggled inside to change the recording paper, I huddled in the lee of the shelter, slapping my hands together to restore circulation. For though we classed it as a warm blizzard, it was not all that warm with the thermometer standing at −15° C.

The return to the hut was a simple business. We had the angle of the wall of the shelter to start us off in the right direction for the hut. Even so there was still enough uncertainty to make us breathe a sigh of relief, when at last we found ourselves fumbling at the door of the hut, to escape that shrieking, tormenting wind.

That night we heard nothing on the radio from the weasel. This was not in itself alarming, since in a dense blizzard it is normal for the receiving antenna to be so charged with static electricity as to make reception impossible.

In the morning the blizzard had blown itself out. Calm reigned once more outside the hut. From the top of the hill we saw that the sea ice was still in to the horizon so we presumed our comrades were safe, and guessed rightly that they were taking advantage of the fine weather to make their run westward.

Lépineux, going to the garage to check the battery charger, was horrified to find the three surviving pups of Ifaut lying stiff and apparently lifeless with their jaws locked on black and distended tongues. In next to no time we had them in a box in the warmth of the hut for Rivolier to diagnose what had happened to them. There didn't seem to be much hope for them. Their little bodies were cold and rigid and they were barely breathing. Of the three, only Sandra showed any sign of life. Rivolier presumed that they had been poisoned by the fumes of the gas-driven battery charger and treated them accordingly.

'The problem is,' explained Rivolier, 'I have to give them an injection of strychnine to stimulate their hearts. I know the dose for a man, but for creatures as small as these I haven't an idea. It's well possible that the dose I give them will kill them.'

We glumly nodded our assent. They looked dead anyway. The injections given we left them and sat down to eat. We were all attached to the three pups and were feeling sad. There did not seem to be much hope for them.

A whimper from outside sent us hurrying to them. Sandra was on her feet, groggily trying to climb out of the box. A little later there was a thump and another whimper. This time it was Bora falling out of the box. An hour later the three of them were wandering unsteadily about the floor of the hut apparently none the worse for their adventure except for the possession of three first-class headaches evidenced by their pawing at their heads in a puzzled manner.

Two days later we were seven at the base again when the weasel rolled to a halt outside the hut after a round trip of one hundred and sixty miles. In that they had not been able to follow the Emperors northward to their feeding grounds the trip had been unsuccessful. But they had made a successful run as far as the Endurance Glacier in the west, where they stored their excess fuel for a major journey later in the year. More important, they had familiarized themselves with weasel travel on the sea ice under local conditions, and this knowledge was going to stand us in good stead when we made our mid-winter journey in a month's time.

5

Cold and Darkness

There will be little said of the dogs in this chapter. It describes a little epic in which the weasel played the leading role and, although I champion the dogs, I must admit that in this period I learned, if not to love the machine, at least to respect it.

Following the disastrous fire at Port Martin and the establishment of us seven at Pointe Géologie with stores for three men for a year to spread among seven, Marret decided that a trip to the burnt-out base of Port Martin in search of food and equipment was essential if we were to attempt to function as a serious Antarctic group. At Port Martin, buried in the snowdrifts, were dumps of food and equipment, which had been spared from the fire, and which we needed very badly. Furthermore, at Port Martin, abandoned after the fire, were three weasels. They had been driven up on the rocks and closed down. If we could succeed in getting these machines in running order we could use them to haul back to our camp at Ile des Pétrels the food and equipment we hoped to salvage from the snowdrifts of Port Martin.

The general plan formulated by Marret was quite simple and logical. Four of us were to go to Port Martin in Hirondelle, our one and only weasel. On our arrival, all that had to be done was to dig out the three weasels there, get their engines operating, then having dug out all the stores we could find, load the gear on to sledges and tow the sledges back to Ile des Pétrels with the weasels.

There were, however, one or two complicating factors. We were short of gasoline for the trip. This, if for no other reason, prevented travel on the plateau, where it would be necessary to make a wide detour southwards to avoid the heavy crevassing at the roots of two large glaciers which lay between us and Port Martin. So the only route available to us was the frozen sea, the same unstable medium of travel that I have already described. The time chosen was midwinter, in the depths of the Antarctic winter when there is no daylight. The temperature is at its lowest and the blizzard screams in fury from the icy wastes of the polar plateau. This was advantageous in that the sea ice was at its stablest, but disadvantageous in the grim travelling conditions that a winter journey must entail.

We had all of us, at one time or another, tried to start the frozen motor of a cold weasel and cursed the obstinacy of the unresponding machinery. Those motors of the abandoned weasels must be damned cold now that six months had passed since they last turned over. Vincent, our cheery and indomitable mechanic, mentioned this to Marret.

'Do you really think we can get those motors going?'

In Marret's reply was embodied the driving spirit that characterized the whole of the midwinter journey to Port Martin.

'We have to.'

The dogs played a small part in the venture too. The first obstacle between us and Port Martin was the snout of the Terra Nova Glacier which projected from the land twenty-five miles out to sea, where it joined the field of hummocks that had barred the way northward on the last weasel trip. The glacier snout presented a continuous wall of ice cliffs two hundred feet high, made up a of solid ice tongue and liberated icebergs. What we needed was to find a passage through the glacier tongue somewhere between the land and the hummock field. So for some days Vincent and I worked along the glacier tongue with a dog team looking for a passage, on day trips from the hut. We had not success until one day, just when it was time to turn back, we ventured into a blind bay of icebergs, not really expecting to find anything, since hereabouts the glacier tongue appeared to present an impenetrable wall. We turned into a narrow cleft between two frozen-in icebergs, so narrow that it was masked by broken ice, and in rounding the corner we found it opened into a wide passage that looked more hopeful than anything that we had seen yet. The surface was very bad, being hummocky and riven into many leads created by the tremendous pressures exerted by the moving bergs. We advanced, and as we did the passage widened. Half a mile farther we halted, and before us to the east the road to Port Martin lay open over the sea ice with the worst of the glacier behind us.

The passage we wanted, though by no means an easy one, was ours to use. That is, of course, if Marret considered he could work our weasel through it. We were not sufficiently experienced to decide that. Very happily we turned and ran for the base with the dogs pulling merrily in their harnesses.

There was a period of preparations at the hut. There were very many things to be considered, checked and prepared, before a group of four men could venture forth into the Antarctic winter for a month. All gear had to be as near perfect as our ingenuity and experience could provide. Just sufficient gear had to be taken and each item had to be carefully considered to get the maximum of efficiency compatible with the minimum of weight.

While these preparations were afoot a tragedy was being enacted in the dog lines.

It began when Helen, the bitch of Boss's team, was mated with Astro.

Old, scarred Boss, whose whole authority rested on his ancient prestige, felt the situation keenly. There was dejected shame in his attitude. His young and high-spirited team seemed delighted with this unpunished transgression by Astro.

It could have passed had not the despised Pomme, whom any of the team could terrorize with impunity, sensing Boss's dejection, begun a series of tentative attacks. Finding Boss's defence half-hearted, he swung in in full battle. Waking from his mood of impotent helplessness Boss returned the offensive and a marathon battle began. The team were beside themselves with excitement.

Backwards and forwards rolled the two combatants; Boss swift and sure, slashing and cutting, each quick movement drawing blood, Pomme heavy and blundering but tireless in the flush of his youth.

Though Boss was undoubtedly winning on points, he was unable to seriously hurt the big Labrador cross through its matted fur. But through ineffective in his tactics, every now and then Pomme was able to sink his fangs into Boss. And Pomme for all his ungainliness was a very powerful dog. But what was worse for Boss was that he was physically incapable of a long sustained fight. He needed a swift decisive battle to win, and every minute the combat continued so his hope of victory diminished. In the breaks he stood gasping with blood staining the froth about his jaws and blood dripping from his wounds. Then, as soon as he recovered his breath, he would launch his tired old body against Pomme once more.

It was in such a breathing space that the tragedy occurred. The team were tied on individual chains along a centre trace while the ends of the centre trace were securely tied to steel pins driven into the rock. The concerted leaping of the whole team against their chains in their excitement broke out a pin at one end of the centre trace. The whole team of blood-mad dogs, now free, closed in on the two fighters.

I caught a glimpse of Boss's expression as the eight big powerful young dogs fell on him. I had only an inkling of what must follow, but Boss knew.

He sank down, belly to the ground, to protect his soft underside, and with his lips drawn back over his broken teeth prepared to defend himself. Then he was hidden by a mass of snarling and snapping dogs, each determined to repay the old leader for the beatings of the past.

They had no fear of him now. It was the end of Boss. Had I left him there a few minutes longer they would have certainly killed him. Perhaps it would have been as well that way, because what I succeeded in pulling clear of the cruel fangs was no longer Boss but a poor tattered remnant in spirit and body of the grand old dog we had all known so well. They had killed his spirit and his pride, it would have been better if they had taken his life as well.

Meanwhile the preparations for the winter journey eastward neared completion.

We left the weasel, Hirondelle, with sledge attached on the bay ice below the camp. Everything was tuned to finality; the sledge was loaded with gear and food, our sleeping-bags were stowed in the cabin of the weasel, and last touch of all, the astro compass was mounted in front of the navigation trap of the machine. There was nothing to hold us at the hut; all was ready for departure.

Nothing except the date, the twenty-second of June, which is midwinter's day in the Antarctic and has always been traditionally celebrated. With our limited resources the hut was a bare and restricted place, comfortable enough in a utilitarian way, but hardly the perfect setting for the party of the year. Something had to be done about it, so we rummaged among our belongings for decorations. The only flags we possessed were our red marker pennants used as trail

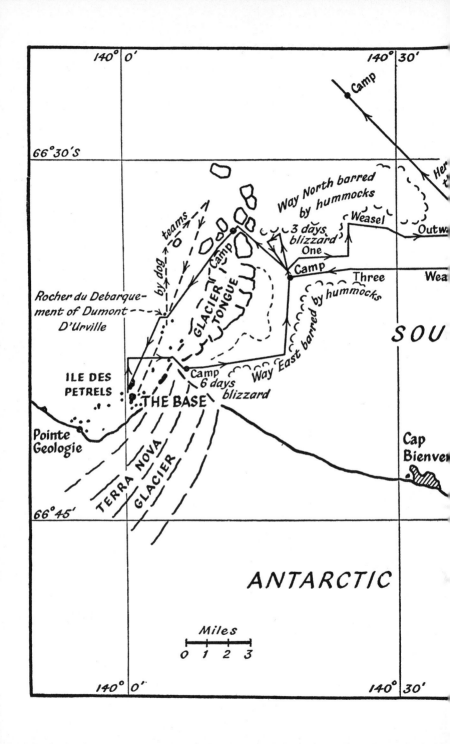

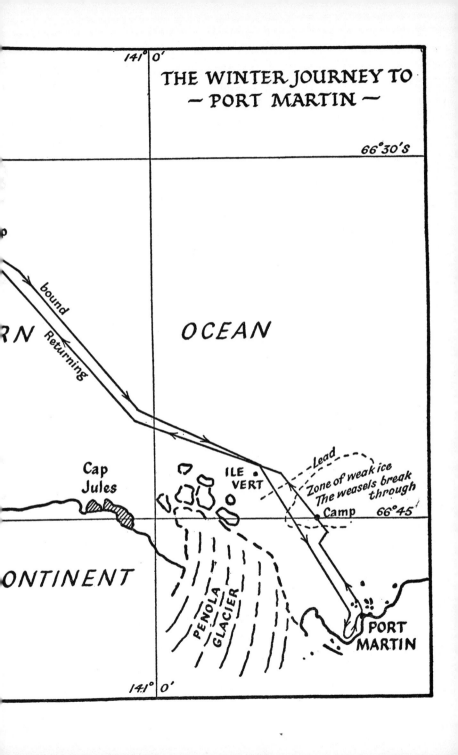

THE WINTER JOURNEY TO
— PORT MARTIN —

markers, but of these we had plenty and the hut was festooned with them. A casual visitor could be pardoned for mistaking the nationality of the expedition. A tent liner of white cloth was hung from the rafters above the table to hide the bare wood of the ceiling. A roll of green canvas ran down the hut side to hide the bunks. Using odd bits of green canvas as leaves and with paper flowers made from our stock of toilet paper Vincent produced our floral decorations. Lépineux and Rivolier, our best cooks, produced the food that was to grace our table while Prévost, forgetting his biological studies for a few hours, did duty as a pastry-cook.

It was more like a meal in a submarine than a hut, but despite the restricted space caused by our decorations, it was a cheering change of scene from our normal hut surroundings. Each one of us had dug deep into his poor supply of clothing for his gayest and cleanest garments. It was warm and merry in the hut that night while outside the wind whistled and the drift snow went sheeting past.

The table was loaded with good food and in the centre stood our greatest treasure—our one and only bottle of champagne. Around the table were the seven gayest men in that sector of the Antarctic, each determined to honour the food and wine to the best of his capabilities. Four of those men were perhaps a little more determined than the others, because in a few hours' time they would be leaving in the weasel to go out into the Antarctic winter for a month on a difficult and hazardous mission. The party got under way decorously enough, the rare abundance of fine food saw to that. It was too good after our normal camp fare to be treated irreverently. But as the edge wore off our appetites, conversation became more animated and the corks came off our wine bottles. There was a moment of shocked silence as Marret accidentally spilled his one and only glass of champagne.

'Anyone can have champage to drink,' he remarked. 'True wealth is having champagne to waste.'

We had always had a bottle of Vitamin C tablets on the table at meals but in the fervour of creative cooking Rivolier had forgotten to put them out. Someone drew his attention to the fact. He disappeared for a moment and returned with the bottle containing the year's supply. With a noble gesture he scattered the contents across the table announcing grandly: 'Never let it be said that any man lacked Vitamin C while I am doctor.'

Georges Lépineux was controller of our groceries and had jealously guarded our food stores to stretch them out as long as possible, so jealously that his control verged on parsimony. Georges watched this magnanimity and was impressed. So when someone remarked that there was no sugar on the table he rose, and copied Rivolier's gesture with an equally grand supply of sugar. This uncustomary generosity left him feeling uncomfortable; not so uncomfortable, however, as the rest of us delving for sugar in the back of our necks.

There was then a suggestion that the dogs must be having a dull midwinter's day and that they should all be brought into the hut with us. I shuddered at the mental picture that presented. Twenty dogs would be brawling, eating, stealing, and being sick in the narrow confines of the hut with we men seeking refuge on the table. Fortunately saner counsel prevailed so the invitation was only extended to Paton and the three small pups.

A little later a wandering Emperor penguin was invited inside and joined us. He stood solemnly at the end of the table and viewed the proceedings with a disapproving eye. To cheer him up he was offered a spoonful of brandy and two Vitamin C pills. The effect of this was startling. The previously dignified and, no doubt, teetotal bird began to behave in a manner that left no doubt about his condition. A fighting drunk if I ever saw one. With raucous cries he chased the pups about the floor and when all pups were hiding, trembling with fear, he turned his aggression on the men.

Very regretfully we were obliged to show our new friend the door.

Eat, drink and be merry for tomorrow we freeze.

Six hours later, Marret, Duhamel and I walked down the ice slope to the weasel where we found the efficient Vincent had the motor turning over. We clambered inside. Marret went to the driver's seat and I went to the navigation trap. The motor revved up as the machine strained against the weight of the heavily loaded sledge and then we were under way. The winter journey to Port Martin had begun.

As Hirondelle headed out between the islands we had a last salute from the base. Every husky in the camp pointed his muzzle to the sky and howled. The other men still slept. Jupiter was shining bright and clear on the northern horizon, so taking our direction from that planet we steered north and east to the glacier passage.

Although it was midwinter and at noon the sun was still below the horizon we could count on several hours of light when dawn and twilight merged into one. We were relying on this period of light to negotiate the tricky and narrow passage through the glacier tongue. It is difficult to describe the glacier passage. Imagine a field of closely packed icebergs, joined by a floor of frozen sea water, with a narrow path existing tortuously between them for a mile. The surface was twisted and broken up by the movement of the icebergs so that crevasses and leads were many; while the tremendous pressures exerted by the billions of tons of ice in the glacier had twisted the sea ice into a nightmare of pinnacles and depressions. Over this chaotic ice lay a mantle of soft fresh snow hiding the leads. On either side of this narrow and winding corridor frowned the hundred-foot-high walls of ice of the bergs. If one of those bergs rolled while the weasel was in the passage it would spell the end of the venture . . . definitely. At the entrance to the passage we saw a dark ungainly shape lying alongside an open lead.

A seal, the first in months! It represented three days' food for the dogs. The weasel halted. A man got out. He walked across to the seal, cocking a heavy calibre pistol as he walked. There was a shot that echoed in the stillness of the glacier tongue. The man walked back to the weasel, holding his hand inside the hood of his parka to warm it up, for it had become frostbitten in the short period he took off his glove to fire the pistol.

We did not feel the cold as we worked the weasel through the glacier tongue, although it was very cold; there was too much hard work to do. Every fifty yards we had to stop the weasel as the man walking ahead, probing with an ice axe, found a fresh crevasse hidden under the mantling snow. A bridge had to be built each time with timbers carried on the weasel, the weasel driven across, the bridge dismantled and stowed on the weasel and the laborious march continued to the next lead. It was late in the afternoon when the weasel stood on the other side of the glacier on level sea ice, facing eastward towards Port Martin with the passage behind us.

A blizzard struck the next day. The temperature was —25° C. and the wind came screaming down from the icy plateau at seventy miles an hour, carrying with it drift snow so dense that visibility was cut to one yard. We began to have an inkling of what winter travel could be like. It was uncomfortable huddled in the weasel cabin but heaven compared to conditions outside. To leave the shelter of the weasel was a laborious operation and one not carried out unless strictly necessary. One trip was important and that was to make a tour of the immediate vicinity of the weasel to check on the condition of the sea ice on which it was standing. We were very conscious of the fact that only a yard of ice separated us from some very deep, dark and very cold water. Our first inspection was made by Duhamel, who after examining behind the weasel, reported that the ice had cracked, creating a new lead. We advanced the weasel a few yards to be clear of this and then examined what lay immediately ahead. A few yards further on was a second open lead, and worse still the edges of the lead were moving up and down with the ocean swell. Not very encouraging information this, for moving ice is dangerous ice. But there was little we could do to improve our situation except sit where we were and hope for the best. Under the present conditions the glacier passage was no longer negotiable, and, even had we wished it, retreat to the Ile des Pétrels was out of the question. For the moment there was nothing we could do except make ourselves as comfortable as possible in the weasel cabin.

The weasel bucked under the onslaught of the wind, and the world outside was an impenetrable mass of swirling snow. Inside the cabin of the weasel we lay in our sleeping bags, watching the walls whiten as our breath condensed upon them with the hoar-frost crystals growing longer and longer. It was like living in the interior of a very efficient refrigerator.

The next day the wind dropped and the temperature rose alarmingly. The sky was heavy with cloud and a light snow-fall continued all day. Visibility was limited to fifty yards with everything in the half-light merged; snow, ice, sky and icebergs joined into a uniform grey white. In weather like this we were unable to travel, for being so close to the South Magnetic Pole a magnetic compass was useless and we were dependent on the sun, moon, or stars for direction. Without these we could not steer a course. This day was a rarity, fortunately. The temperature was exceedingly high for that season, a heat wave in fact, with the thermometer standing at a mere $-2°$ C. We were able to lounge in the cabin with the doors wide open, reading or wondering just what adverse

effect this sudden rise in temperature would have on the
sea ice. Despite our relative comfort we would have preferred it to stay cold.

At this stage the plan was that the dog teams would follow
our tracks out from Ile des Pétrels, bringing with them
Vincent, the fourth member of our party, and then the dogs
and the weasel would head northward together. The weasel
would halt at a strategic point to act as a base, while the dog
teams would make a quick probe farther north in an attempt
to solve the mystery of the feeding grounds of the Emperor
penguins. This done the dogs would return to Ile des Pétrels.
The weasel would then continue on to Port Martin. This
run of bad weather was threatening to prevent these projects.

The next day the temperature fell but visibility remained
very much the same. By radio we learnt from the Base that
Prévost and Vincent had left with the dog team following
the edge of the glacier. Duhamel and I walked through the
glacier passage to meet them at the other side. For quite
some time we could hear Prévost's commands to the dogs
before we saw a line of moving black dots near the glacier
edge in the grey half-light.

As there was no immediate hope of moving on in such
poor visibility, Prévost returned to Ile des Pétrels with the
dogs, leaving Vincent with us. We loaded the carcass of the
seal we had killed two days earlier on to his sledge before he
left. Before Vincent's arrival, with only three of us sleeping
in the weasel cabin, it had been a squeeze to find room for
three sleeping bags, but now we were four it was a tight fit.
It meant that one man had to sleep across the engine. Since
Marret and Vincent were the two smallest, they took it in
turns with that uncomfortable bed.

The weather continued to prejudice the enterprise. We
were prevented from advancing each day by either blizzard
or bad visibility. The hope of working the dog search north
in co-operation with the weasel was fading fast as day fol-

lowed day with the weasel immobilized. Five days went by and we were obliged to ask the base to make a second trip to us with the dog teams, to bring out food and fuel to replace that already used, so that we might start fully provisioned on the main journey. Prévost and Rivolier arrived with Bjorn's team, bringing with them the supplies demanded. This was to be the last time we were to see them for a month, so while Marret chatted with Rivolier and Prévost giving them final instructions for the running of the base in his absence, I had a last few words with the dogs.

Silly old Bjorn and the gentle Ifaut seemed glad to see me again. Fram was as afraid of Bjorn as ever; though he edged over to be patted a growl from Bjorn sent him cowering back against the sledge. Maru, the terror of the penguin rookery, seemed puzzled. He was forever looking to left and right wondering why there was no penguins here. Milk and Tiki, the two inseparables, were standing together licking each other's chops in affection and growling half in defiance and half in fear at Fram. One could never feel the same way towards the cold mass of the weasel as one did to these warm-blooded creatures. I gave them a last pat before they returned and asked Rivolier to keep a special eye on poor old Boss. Then, with a crack of the whip, the team and sledge were off on their way through the glacier passage homeward, with the dogs straining at their traces, spurred by the thought of returning to their idea of perfect comfort, the dog lines at base.

We had a warm blizzard again but on the twenty-ninth of June the weather broke. Without regret we turned the weasel northward and broke out from the glacier camp.

The first day was heavy going. We found ourselves working through a zone of hummocky ice. Here the surface was anything but smooth; the early sea ice had been broken in a gale so that the shattered sections of ice piled up pell-mell in the bay, some were rafted on to others while some floes were frozen vertically in place. The whole presented an effect of distortion and confusion. Great snowdrifts had built up amid this chaos of blue ice and it was no longer a case of selecting a route for the weasel but of making one with picks and shovels.

We were advancing at very much less than a walking pace, so the thought that this condition would persist all the way to Port Martin was a worrying one, since our small fuel reserves would not be able to cope with the unexpected low-gear work.

It was slow work with one man walking ahead in the bitter cold by the light of the weasel headlights and a half moon, trying to pick the easiest road. Behind him the other three followed with the weasel, breaking down and smoothing the track with picks and shovels. Here and there they would be obliged to hew a path through ice walls and snowdrifts several yards high to permit the weasel to advance. We were using the moon to steer by, but it was difficult to maintain a course twisting and turning in that maze of ice. There was just enough wind coming away from the south to chill one to the bone the moment one stood still and with it came a light spraying of fine, drifting snow. But it was here, at a time of personal discomfort and travelling difficulties, that I found my most vivid impression of this year in Antarctica. I had been walking ahead of the weasel, choosing a route, and paused to look back at the group following me.

It was a scene of desolation; of an unearthliness not of this planet but rather of the face of the moon. As far as the eye could see under the weak light was a field of fantastic ice shapes, with the drift snow swirling eerily among the pinnacles of ice and dunes of snow beneath the cold light of the moon. There was but one form of life here, all else was dead and sterile; but that was as fantastic as its surroundings: the weasel with its engine revving and roaring as it clambered clumsily among the storm-shattered floes. The weasel headlights were like two great eyes, one moment pointed at the ground and the next staring skywards. This was the earth at its inception, at the beginning of time, with the weasel some great prehistoric beast stalking its prey by the full of the moon.

This was a scene that time had forgotten.

The hummocks seemed endless. We began to wonder whether there was any reason to expect a change, and began to believe that we would be obliged to hack a road with pick and shovel all the way to Port Martin. Every now and then the weasel would be pulled brutally to a halt as the sledge fouled on a pinnacle of ice. We would hack away the obstruction with picks before we could go on. It was my turn ahead and I was beginning to suspect that the disturbed surface was becoming less severe, but said nothing to the others since already we had encountered several small patches of better going, which, just as we were congratulating ourselves on having escaped, would end abruptly in further hummocks. Ten minutes later I climbed over a great drift and found myself walking on a level uniform surface with the hummocks left behind me. The road ahead lay open. We all clambered aboard the weasel and began to run northward at fine speed. We camped when the gathering clouds obscured the moon, for without a moon to steer by we had no way of knowing direction.

Our constant enemy, the blizzard, struck again. We huddled in the weasel cabin, listening to the wind shrieking outside, and feeling the machine jolt with the savage fury of the blizzard. Each hoped that there would be no cause for him to venture out of the comparative comfort of the cabin into the cold hell raging outside. 'Comparative' indeed. The cabin was pervaded by an insidious cold that began by numbing the hands and feet then gradually sent its icy fingers searching deeper towards the centre of the body. To touch anything, even the outside of a sleeping-bag, was painful. We sat up in our sleeping-bags and talked or dozed, wriggling our feet to restore circulation. But, unpleasant as these conditions may sound, they were luxury to the icy viciousness that clamoured outside.

We were five weary and cheerless days there, waiting helplessly for the elements to calm. Five days camped on a yard thick piece of ice with a thousand fathoms of cold dark water below it, and with many miles between us and solid land. Five days, in which from time to time each man was obliged to forsake the warmth of his sleeping-bag and the shelter of the cabin, themselves no perfect comfort, and go out into the blizzard to answer a call of nature. This simple operation entailed a small expedition in itself, and was not one that was lightly undertaken. Though the unfortunate so pressed was the butt of shafts of humour from his companions, there was a sense of fellow sympathy behind their witticisms. He rigged himself up as completely as possible and tied down his gloves on his wrists before he dived out of the door. Once outside he found himself alone in a shrieking, blinding nightmare of flying snow, unable to stand in that wind, obliged to crawl until he found a corner a little more sheltered than the rest.

When the weather eventually broke we struck north-west to the seaward end of the glacier tongue, where the last bergs, seperated from the main body of the river of ice, stood as sheer-fronted snowy islands in a field of shattered ice. We thought it possible that here the movement of these free bergs might break the sea ice sufficiently to allow the Emperors to enter the sea in search of food. Some three miles from the nearest we were forced to halt the weasel by a barrier of distorted ice. From there we proceeded on foot.

Marret went off alone towards the most distant berg, while Duhamel and I headed in a more southerly direction towards a group of several. Vincent remained alone with the weasel. The search was fruitless. All bergs were frozen solidly into the sea ice, neither seal nor penguin could hope to find a crack large enough to squeeze in or out of the water. The whole area was completely lifeless and all we found were some tracks of the big penguins, deeply imprinted in soft new snow, still heading northwards towards the distant open water. We were now some twenty-five miles from the nearest land. Somewhere to the north was a zone where the ice was shattered by the storms and the frost smoke hung like a pall over the dark black water. That was where those Emperor tracks were leading.

The indomitable Marret, after checking our meagre fuel supply, decided to make a last effort to put the search farther north before turning on our main objective, Port Martin. It was once again a weary, unrewarding business. We encountered the same continuous zone of hummocks that had barred our way before. Our track on the chart was generally eastward, with a series of fingers pointing northward where at intervals we had tried to push in that direction before being forced over east by that ever-present barrier of shattered ice. At last, towards midnight, our luck changed when a turn to the north opened up into a zone of only light hummocks. We went on for six hours, dodging and swerving to avoid ice pinnacles and big snow drifts but always steadily wearing away to the north. The weasel under way under these conditions is like a ship at sea. The driver is crouched in the driving seat against the engine peering through an iced and frosted windscreen. The navigator stands on the engine cover with his head and shoulders out through the navigation trap, watching the track ahead and periodically shouting changes of direction or warnings to the driver. Behind them in the cabin are the two passengers, curled up in as much comfort as the jolting vehicle allows, but ready to spring into action if needed. The navigator curses as he tries to turn the frozen setting screws of the astro compass with gloved hands and to pick up the pale disc of the moon through its frosted sights. At the same time he shouts down instructions to the driver.

'Left . . . Hard left . . .! A little more . . . Steady . . . On course.'

'Right . . . Hard right . . . Hard right!' As a wall of broken ice looms up out of the gloom ahead.

We were forging ahead at a steady seven miles an hour on what appeared to be a perfectly level sheet of sea ice, when suddenly a seal's head popped up dead ahead almost under the machine in the headlights, peering at the weasal thundering at him. He gave a disgusted snort and disappeared. It happened so quickly that I might have imagined it save for the cloud of his condensed breath that still hung in the air. Where a seal can come up a weasel can easily go down, so there was an anxious moment or two after I screamed down 'Full speed!' till the danger was passed. We stopped the weasal and went back to investigate. A refrozen lead ran across the weasel track and, where the track crossed it, there was a neat round hole in the new ice that the seal had chewed out and kept open by the same means ever since. We left a flag on a bamboo to mark the spot against our return.

Once again the moon played us false and hid her shy face in the gathering clouds. Once more we were obliged to halt through lack of a means of determining direction. We were now very far from land, and the ice immediately ahead was little more than a month old. Behind us there were the familiar signs and portents of a new blizzard. It was a very apprehensive group that made camp that night, conscious of the instability of the ice and the many trackless miles of it that lay between us and the nearest solid land. The sky was completely overcast. The wind was rising and a fine snow had begun to fall.

To push our reconnaissance a few miles farther a man went ahead on foot, while the other three cooked a meal. He carried an electric torch to light his way and the headlights of the weasel would guide him back. He strode off into the icy darkness, in the vain hope that somewhere ahead were tracks of the Emperor penguins.

The sum total of absolute loneliness is one man, on foot, walking northward over the ice in the middle of the Antarctic winter. Ahead of him are the trackless wastes of a frozen sea leading out through shattered floes to the storm-lashed open water, while behind him is a vast, icy unpeopled continent. His three companions in the weasel form his only link with the living world. As he walks slowly forward, stumbling over ridges of ice, he expects and finds nothing. After two miles with nothing found he turns back. A momentary panic seizes him as he finds he can no longer see the weasel headlights. Then he begins to walk slowly back, following the faint imprints of his feet on the surface of the snow, hoping that the falling snow will not hide them before he sees the weasel again.

Two hours later he is back, and we four are grouped together at the weasel. We had pushed our search for the Emperors as far as our resources could stand; little petrol remained above the bare essential to take us on to Port Martin. We felt we could, with honour, turn our backs on the unsolved problem and head direct for Port Martin. Our present position was untenable, we were too far from land for safety. So after a few hours' sleep waiting for the little light that comes when dawn and twilight meet at noon, we commenced our run back to land. It was still snowing with a fair wind and the sky was completely overcast when we got under way. The only way we had of finding our way back was to follow the faint vestiges of the weasel's outward track. The falling snow had completely hidden it for most of the way. It was a trying affair; visibility was limited to a hundred yards. Sky and snow met as a blank wall, and a dark spot of grease dropped off the weasel track could be what it really was, or what our straining eyes insisted it was, a great dark mass of rock twenty miles away. It was a great relief when a little fluttering red flag loomed up out of the white murk. This was the lead where we had seen the seal, and the flag proof that we were still following our outward route. We finally camped, still well away from land, where our outward track had turned northward from the easterly course towards Port Martin. Once more we had only a few hours' sleep before we found the clouds were breaking and several stars could be seen. Kind, friendly stars these, whose little points of light were all we needed to head turn our weasel toward Port Martin and keep it there.

This was to be a fine day's run. Previously, we had won every mile dearly through shattered ice fields, hummocks, and sastrugi. Now for the first time a clear and smooth route lay ahead. The weasel engine, which had been revving and roaring as it laboured over the earlier rough going, settled down to an even whine and the miles began to drop away steadily behind us. The stars disappeared as the midday dawn lit the sky. At last ahead we saw a small, black island in the distance. This was Ile Vert, only thirteen miles north of Port Martin. Not so encouraging was a line of blizzard stretching like a wall behind Ile Vert. Somewhere behind that barrier of snow was Port Martin. Behind us in the north-west it was fine and clear. This was the line of demarcation between the Port Martin world and the world of the sea ice. Just on the fine weather side of that line we could see Ile Vert.

We entered the blizzard zone and tried to run down the direct course to Port Martin on dead reckoning. It was a queer sensation for me, at the navigation trap, heading into the blizzard. I could not see the surface of the sea ice, only the masses of snow swirling past at high speed. As a result I had an impression of travelling at very high speed, and each time the weasel changed course, I found myself leaning

against the turn, holding grimly to the superstructure, fearful that the weasel would roll over. It was only by looking
at the speedometer that I could convince myself that our
speed was not the hundred miles an hour it seemed, but a
modest five.

We retreated out of the blizzard. A little later we tried
again. We drove back into the driving, blinding snow. Marret was directing from the navigation trap. Suddenly he
screamed down to Vincent who was driving.

'Top speed! Lead!'

The engine roared, the weasel surged ahead, but at the
same time the stern slumped, the tracks scrambled and then
with a lurch we were once more on an even keel driving
ahead. We had run across a wide lead, unperceived in the
dense drift, and only the speed of the weasel had jumped it
across, breaking through as we went but scrambling out of
the other side among shattered ice. This blind running was
pushing our luck too far. We crawled out of the blizzard
zone and sheltered at Ile Vert.

I remember it seemed very cold there, stamping about on
the ice beside the weasel and waiting for a meal to be
cooked. The frost rime lay thick and heavy on the men's
beards. I breathed against my glove and frost appeared on it
like a slap from a paint brush charged with white paint. I
found myself idly speculating how long a man would stay
alive if he were alone here without food or shelter, even
clothed as heavily as I was. If he could keep moving he
would stay warm, but when he stopped the cold would claim
him. Probably he would last one or two days before he
finally drifted off into a numbed sleep from which there
would be no awakening.

The blizzard eased two hours later and we were able to
go on. I navigated until we could see black rock and looming coastal ice cliffs through breaks in the drifting snow.
I knew we were in the immediate locality of Port Martin

A meal in the hut, showing Vincent, Rivolier and Duhamel,
who is partly hidden

The destruction of a
first-class Antarctic
station. Port Martin
afire in a 50-knot
wind

Above: A land of cold silence

Emperor penguins move in a slow dignified walk

Adelie penguin and chick

Credit: A.N.A

Reconnaissance with the dog teams. The camp at Ile Fram

Roald, once the pet of the station, takes a poor view of dog sledging.

Bjorn's team in characteristic poses. Bjorn, Fram (taking his
ease), Maru (watching penguins), Milk and Tiki

Husky mother and son. Yacka with one of her pups

Aspirin—he made only one se[n] journey and came home riding o[n] sledge. His station on the barge the galley was more to his liking pulling a sledge

Bjorn about to attack Seismo

Credit: A.N.A.

Wild

Milk

Credit: A.N.A.R.E.

The Emperor penguin rookery
in the autumn

Emperors admiring their chick

Life returns with the sun
Adelie penguins in foreground

Credit: *A.N.A.R.E.*

The chicks are formed in nurseries under a few adults while both
parents go fishing to feed their chick

The snow petrel, the
white wraith of a white
land, epitomizes the wild
beauty of the south

Credit: A.N.A.R.E.

The weasel train heading westward on the plateau

Weasel with one foot down. Marret directing salvage

Credit: A.N.A.R.E.

Dog team following the weasels westward in drifting snow

Fram

Flensing a Weddel seal. We needed a seal every
three days to feed our dogs and ourselves

Credit: A.N.A.R.E.

Seismo—the little tough

Settling down for the night on the plateau. Note the ice formed
in Astro's fur

Upper right: Ifaut looked small, gentle and out of place among
the dogs

Lower right: Bjorn uncovers a frozen block of seal meat for
breakfast

The bay at Ile des Pétrels in the early autumn. Terra Nova Glacier
in the background

but that was all. Marret, who had spent a year at Port Martin two years ago, took over from me. After two years he still remembered groping around the station area in a blizzard and from his memory directed us. After a quarter of an hour he called out 'Stop!' The burnt-out hut, he told us, was thirty yards away to our left. At that moment the drift cleared and we saw it.

The weasel was pulled to a halt among the stark, twisted and fire-blackened embers of what had been a fine base. It so happened that I was the only one of us who had seen the base immediately after the fire and knew what to expect. For the others, they had last seen a great warm hut, filled with modern comforts and noisy with friendly chatter and music. Though they realized the base had been completely destroyed I do not think that they expected quite the ruin that was there. A few twisted and blackened pieces of ironwork, sticking at crazy angles from the snow, wireless masts awry with severed lines flying in the wind, a few cases here and there, and then ruin, black ruin all about them, was all that remained of a once proud station. Superimposed on the picture I have drawn the pale cold light of a dying moon and drift snow swirling and whispering among the broken skeletons of steel, and you have a picture of what awaited us at journey's end.

Duhamel was first out of the weasel, running across to look more closely at it. He turned, exclaiming to Marret, 'What a hell of a place you have brought us to!'

There was little time wasted comparing impressions. Our first concern was to check whether the tiny refuge hut which had been spared by the fire was still habitable. It seemed to be filled with snow. We were unable to force open the door, so smashed in the window and dug our way in through the tough, packed snow. Once in, we shovelled the tiny hut clear of snow. It seemed no time before we had the stove alight and were huddled around it drinking a mug of steaming cocoa, and remarking on what luxury it was to be inside a hut, no matter how small, compared with the narrow, unsympathetic confines of the weasel.

The next morning we found the three abandoned weasels where they had been run up on the rocks and closed down six months ago. The drift snow had driven through even the minutest of holes to pack the insides of the cabins in a rock-like mass. The tracks had melted into the ice and were frozen in, while great mounds of rock-like drift had formed against the machines. The temperature was —25° C. and a keen wind was blowing. Ahead of Vincent lay the task of putting those three machines in running order. We could help in the beginning. First we had to break open the cabin door, then laboriously chip the ice away from the driving seat. It was a tunnelling operation, working through the door down over the seat to the driving controls. This done with picks and crowbars, we prized the steel tracks out of their cases of ice, breaking each element clear until the tracks were free. Then, with Hirondelle we towed this, the first of the recovered weasels, as close to the refuge hut as possible where Vincent could begin work in earnest.

Where possible one of the others helped him, but most of the work could only be done by him. It was a miserable business. The fine, driven snow had found its way into every cranny of the motor and formed into ice. All that ice had to be chipped away by hand, swept up, and thrown out before he could begin work on the motor itself. In the prevailing temperatures a bare hand placed on metal stuck and the frozen metal burnt as though red hot. Much of the work Vincent had to do could only be done with bare hands working with metal tools. And he worked, day after day, as long as it was humanly possible and beyond the limits I would have set, with that same cheery indomitable grin we had seen so often as he repaired a watch in the warm comfortable hut at Ile des Pétrels.

Meanwhile, apart from helping him, the rest of us were busy enough digging away among the snowdrifts for food and equipment spared by the fire. That is, busy enough when the weather permitted, for the weather was something quite special to the place. Marret, who had spent a year here, had tried to tell us what it was like, but all of us believed only part of his description, for we could not see how so great a difference could exist between points so close together as Port Martin and Ile des Pétrels. We were soon accusing him of understatement. Incessant blizzards shrieked down from the plateau, carrying with them an opaque mass of swirling snow. We found it was quite pointless trying to follow any sort of routine; we were no longer masters of our own destinies. The blizzard ruled us with its icy hand.

Duhamel and I were working at the food dump, digging in the rock-hard drift for buried cases. The wind was rising and the drift snow becoming thicker. I noticed that despite my heavy clothing and the hard physical work I was getting colder. I redoubled my efforts in order to generate more body heat, but the cold was winning. I could not generate as much heat as I was losing. Besides, I was finding it difficult to see. A mask of ice had formed over my face and my eyelids kept freezing together. I felt it was time to find Duhamel, three yards away, and get to the warmth of the tiny hut before we became helpless with ice and frostbite. I hesitated to do this, feeling that if he was still able to work, then I should be too. I met him floundering towards me, a dark shape in the sheeting whiteness. He was in a worse state than I. His face was a mask of ice with his eyes blinded by his frozen eyelids. Not only was he blinded but he had lost a glove trying to clear them and his hand was frostbitten. He was all but helpless and, if alone, would have been in considerable danger. He too, no doubt, had kept going spurred by the same foolish pride in his own fitness that I had had. Clutching each other so as not to be separated by the buffeting of the wind, we stumbled our way back to the little hut, and though we were only two hundred yards from it, we had difficulty in finding it. It was fortunate for both of us that my point of danger with exposure arrived a little later than his. As it was it was our first lesson in the respect due to our master, the blizzard.

A few days later it was blowing worse than usual. We had been working in pairs, in turn, in the recovered weasel. Marret and I, having done several hours there, had returned to warm up in the refuge hut. We covered those thirty yards by crawling, navigating from one microscopic landmark to the next. Here it was the wind-shredded butt of a bamboo protruding from the snow. From there we went to a crushed peach tin. Once that was found, we moved on to a trace of coal and from there floundered against the wall of the tiny hut until we located the door. The other two left the weasel crawling on all fours together. Vincent had one hand on Duhamel's ankle. The first we knew of this was when Duhamel arrived in the hut doorway, frostbitten, near exhausted, and alone. He had lost Vincent in that little distance between hut and weasel. We were getting ready to plunge out into the blizzard in search of him when Vincent came stumbling in. The vicious wind had torn him away from Duhamel, then he had lost his sense of direction. He had crawled around for what had seemed an interminable time until he found himself among the wreckage of the burnt-out main hut. Recognizing this he was able to follow the debris to the refuge hut. These two were tougher, harder, and more experienced than the average man. But over a distance of thirty yards they had barely succeeded in struggling back to the little hut! Such is the blizzard.

We found ourselves settling down to life at Port Martin, each with his own share of the work to do, while the wind and snow did their best to sabotage what had already been done. Settling down as though we had never known any other life than this, we soon grew to accept the fact that our efforts were insignificant in the scale of things at Port Martin. We could spend many hours digging a hole through wind-packed snow into a food stack, only to find in an hour that the hole had been filled by the enemy and the work would have to start again. We would be all huddled about the stove in the tiny hut listening to the shriek of the wind when there would be a slight lull. We would clamber into our heavy clothing and disappear outside, each to his own task, with barely a word spoken. And this would apply to any hour of the day or night, for no period of calm or light wind could be wasted; midnight, midday or the early hours of the morning made little difference.

One compensation was that we could eat what we wished and as much as we wished. There was an abundance of food in cases stacked about the station. All we had to do was to find it. It was rather like a treasure hunt. We had no list of the cases or their contents and until a case was opened we never knew what we would find inside. It could be a spare clutch plate for the weasels or a case of jam. One peculiar coincidence of the search for equipment was that, no matter what the item of equipment was that we required, no sooner would we begin to search for it, than we would find it. More that that, we would find it in just the numerical quantity we required. For example, we badly needed eiderdown parkas for all seven of the party. Starting to prospect about the dump of equipment cases I opened a case and found eiderdown parkas inside. And there were seven of them.

The great moment came when the motor of Coccinelle, the first of the recovered weasels, roared into life after six months of silence. It was an earnest of the fact that, despite the inimical and implacable blizzard, we were advancing towards our ends. A few days later Alfred, the second of them, added his voice and now, where we had arrived with one serviceable weasel, Hirondelle, we now had three. Once started these motors were not allowed to cool down, for there was fuel in abundance here. Every two hours, day or night, in all weather, a man struggled out from the hut, visiting each weasel in turn to run up their motors.

It seemed that we had more work than we could manage. Sledges and stores that had already been dug out ready for departure would be buried again overnight and they would have to be dug out again. At times I feared we were no longer even holding our gains but that the blizzard was defeating us.

Even Vincent was unable to put the fourth weasel in order. He had more than enough to do to maintain the three already running, so the fourth weasel was jacked up on fuel drums and stripped for spare parts. This done, all was ready for our return. All we needed was a few hours of reasonable weather to clear Port Martin, but blizzard seemed to have no intention of giving us that. We nailed up the door of the refuge hut and transferred ourselves to the weasel cabins. Marret and Vincent went to Coccinelle, Duhamel and I took up our quarters in Hirondelle, while Alfred was left vacant. Alfred was spurned for a good reason; despite his attractive exterior he generated deadly carbon monoxide gas within his cabin and had almost claimed Marret as a victim several days previously.

It does not seem a great advance to move thirty yards from a hut to the weasels but it was. It meant that when the weather broke we would save that much good weather to devote to digging out the weasels and sledges and getting under way before the blizzard struck again. It meant also that we had abandoned hut life once more and were again nomads, living in our weasels and ready to travel.

We had three days of continuous blizzard that bound us where we were, thirty yards from the hut. The drift snow built high about the weasels and the sledges loaded with stores vanished altogether. The three weasels were in line abreast with Alfred, the uninhabited, in the center. On a roster we took it in turns to visit Alfred every two hours to turn over his motor. In those three days we saw little of the other two; Duhamel and I were living in our little world in Hirondelle while Marret and Vincent were in theirs in Coccinelle's cabin. The driving snow hid us from each other.

In the waking hours we cooked and ate. Duhamel, a former sailor, told me all the funny stories he could remember. I was struck by the fact that his stories had no national flavour. They were the same stories as those I had listened to underneath the olive groves of Lebanon, under the gum trees of Australia, or in a foxhole in the steaming jungle of New Guinea. The only difference was that the characters had Gallic names. He told me how, as a young sailor, with two of his fellows he had visited a native village in Madagascar famed for its lake containing sacred crocodiles. In bygone times these beasts exacted a toll in human sacrifice. Duhamel and his companions had prevailed upon the headman, after much argument, to let them witness the sacrifice of an ox. When the headman agreed he told them it would cost them five thousand francs, not only to appease the possible wrath of the sacred reptiles for the sacrilege, but also, the 'Capitans' being practical men would understand, to buy the ox. After the necessary ritual dances the cortege including the ox moved down to the lakeside. It was evening and the blazing torches the natives carried threw a lurid light over the sinister stillness of the water. The natives, in full regalia, were in a state of great excitement. They brandished spears and beat drums. The still water seemed latent with the evil it hid; Duhamel could imagine great sinister shapes closing in on the beach beneath its surface. The witch doctor, garishly decorated, blew a shell trumpet and his acolytes beat the surface of the water with their spears. Ripples broke the surface, and half a dozen enormous heads appeared, their jaws agape, showing their awesome jaws in the torch-light. Duhamel glanced nervously at his companions; they were a long way from their ship, and it was not so very long ago that it was not an ox that was flung to these loathsome reptiles. An axe rose and fell with a dull crunch. The next minute two expert native butchers were at work on the carcass. With skilful hands they dismembered the ox, pass-ing the cuts of meat to eager hands waiting behind them. When nothing remained but the head and a pile of uncook-able bones the sacrifice took place. The sacred beasts re-ceived the bones, the meat had long since vanished together with most of the worshippers back to the village. The magic of the moment was spoiled. The crocodiles received their pittance without complaint, no doubt counting themselves lucky in these cynical times to get as much, but watching Duhamel with reminiscent eyes, remembering happier days.

It was a sudden jar from this yarn to find myself due to go out into the cold. It was minus thirty and the wind was blowing more than eighty knots, carrying fine snow so thick it looked as though it could be cut with an axe. This drift snow was so fine it penetrated everything. Even in the sealed cabin a fine powder of it lay over everything including our sleeping-bags. Frost rime, condensed from our breathing and from previous cooking, was half an inch thick on the cabin walls. It was cold inside the cabin, but it was warm in our sleeping-bags. I half crawl out of mine and lean over the engine, pushing aside the outer clothes we have spread over its still warm mass in order to thaw them. After adjusting the controls, I press the starter button and the engine turns over. It runs for ten minutes until the temperature gauge is sufficiently high, then it is cut off. I get into my outer cloth-ing, pummelling my still frozen gloves into shape and wres-tling my feet into hard, icy boots. Duhamel stands by to close the door as I dive out. As I go out the drift swirls in.

I cannot see. The drift is so thick that it is an opaque wall.

I grope my way to Alfred, feeling for the door. There are two wing nuts sealing the door against rubber liners, which have to be undone. Under anything like normal conditions they would take at most a minute to unscrew, but here, with the wind plucking at me, it is fully ten minutes before I have them undone. Getting inside the cabin is a relief. Although there is snow and ice everywhere and further drift is swirling through the imperfectly closed door, at least I have escaped the direct force of the wind. The motor is covered with snow and ice and the instrument panel is hidden. I brush away as much as I can, locate the ignition key and find it will not turn. The alternate heating and chilling of the engine has melted the snow and then refrozen it about the controls. I notice that the last man here has replaced the choke knob with a piece of wire when it became inoperable. After a further ten minutes I manage to get the motor turning over, and while I wait for it to heat up, I brush away as much of the snow about the engine as I can. Those two wing nuts on the door obsess me. I spend the moments of waiting working out a plan to get them on swiftly. I cut the motor, dive out into the open, and begin to battle with the wind to close the door. Despite the plan, the wing nuts keep me cursing for ten minutes. As my hands go numb I find it increasingly difficult to screw them, until finally in desperation I whip off my gloves and screw them on with bare hands. Then back to Hirondelle and comfort with no prospect of a further sortie for another six hours.

Duhamel regards me with disfavour. I know what he is thinking. Did I have to be that clumsy, half filling the cabin with drift snow and bringing cubic feet of it in packed into my clothing? This does not worry me in the least. My main concern is to warm my hands over the engine, and then get back into my sleeping-bag. Strange, I thought, it is not getting your hands frozen that hurts but thawing them out that is really painful. I feel a bit sorry for Duhamel who has all this to go through in two hours' time.

What hurt most was once when I went through this unpleasant ritual only to find when I went to start Alfred's motor that it was still hot. Vincent, operating from his weasel, had been there only a few minutes before. As I struggled once more with the obstinate wing nuts I thought of the wartime posters. 'Is this trip necessary?'

We had four hours of fair weather. We used every minute of it, working like Trojans, to dig the weasels and sledges out of the snow. We managed to get the whole train under way and were on the sea ice half a mile from Port Martin when the blizzard closed down on the train with redoubled fury. Once more we brought the three weasels into line abreasts, each still connected to its train of sledges, and closed down. Duhamel and I were beginning to take an active dislike to Port Martin; it seemed that the place, once having us at its mercy, was reluctant to see us escape. We spoke of this accursed country, and Ile Vert, a bare thirteen miles away, seemed to us the gateway of a new world. We almost believed in the Port Martin ogre we had created, '*Le petit bonhomme du plateau*,' who peeped over the icy rim of the plateau at the ineffectual striving of us human ants, letting us play for a while, then, at his own capricious humour, puffing out his cheeks and blowing down upon us.

Two more days of ceaseless blizzard. If anything it blew harder than ever before. We were obliged to shore up the walls of the weasel with timber, for fear the cabin would be wrenched off by the violence of the wind.

It broke, as even the worst weather must sooner or later. It was a fine feeling as we headed off. At last we were starting on the final phase of the journey; the run home to Ile des Pétrels. Hirondelle was in the lead, Vincent followed driving Coccinelle and Marret brought up the rear in Alfred, the most unreliable of the three weasels. The surface was excellent, only the lightest of sastrugi. I slipped into third gear and we were rolling along at ten miles an hour with the three weasels strung out in line ahead. There was no strain in driving. I lit a cigarette and looked around. True the plateau rim behind Port Martin was fuzzy with an impending blizzard but the way ahead to the north-west looked fine and clear. I began to make mental calculations; thirteen miles to Ile Vert, say at most two hours, then across the bay in front of Penola glacier, add another four hours, we should be off the end of the Terra Nova glacier in twelve hours. . . . Why, it was possible we should roll into camp at Ile des Pétrels before twenty-four hours were out. I looked up at Duhamel at the navigation trap, he held his fingers in the victory sign and grinned. He too was jubiliant, he pointed to Port Martin vanishing astern and grinned again. This was how it should be, rolling along without a care in the world.

Then it happened! The weasel gave a sideways lurch and shuddered to a halt. I leaned out and saw water about the weasel tracks. We had broken through. Duhamel gave the pre-arranged signal for this emergency to Vincent. Vincent slipped his train of sledges and brought Coccinelle on a wide arc to our assistance. Duhamel stood by ready to hook in a steel towing cable. While we were extricating Hirondelle the blizzard behind us closed in.

We were three days making those thirteen miles to Ile Vert. The weasels broke through seven times. Once both Hirondelle and Coccinelle, which was towing Hirondelle, were in the water together and only the presence of the despised Alfred saved the day. The cheerfulnss of our departure was gone; there seemed to be doubt now whether we would be able to get back to Ile des Pétrels; we might yet have to turn back to Port Martin. The only way of advancing was to find a safe route by digging a hole every ten yards, testing the ice with pick and shovel. I shudder to think how many holes I dug in those three days. A sobering thought was that this was the terrain we had gaily charged over in a half blizzard as we came into Port Martin with our single weasel. If we had broken through then . . . !

Abreast of Ile Vert the going became better and we resumed normal travelling, recalling the man on foot ahead. A few miles on we encountered the lead we had jumped on our way in. It was a nasty looking thing four yards wide with a mere film of new ice over the water. We took no chances with it this time. We built a bridge and drove the weasels over it carefully. Alfred's fuel pump went out of action, necessitating a halt while Vincent effected repairs. All mechanical vehicles have souls, in my opinion, and most of them are malignant, like Alfred's. I longed for my friendly dogs.

Then began a fine run homewards. It was then six p.m., and by driving non-stop, apart from enforced halts due to Alfred's malicious eccentricites, we arrived off the end of the Terra Nova glacier at four a.m. the following day. At the end of the Terra Nova was a landmark. We had left a red flag attached to a bamboo to mark the point to turn into the hummocks for the glacier passage. Between it and Ile Vert was a waste of snow and ice, no landmark, nothing except the twinkling stars to guide us on through the darkness of the polar night. When I calculated we should be at the flag we stopped in the darkness. In the light of midday the next day we woke and scanned the horizon and saw it waving proudly, the only friendly thing in the icy landscape.

We felt we were as good as home. Port Martin seemed a long way behind us. All we needed was to press on a little longer. We felt that way until we made radio contact with the base and they informed us that the glacier passage was no longer negotiable, and that we would have to find a new one. Were we to fail now that we were so close to home, just because the glacier had chosen to shudder in its bed?

We engaged the weasels in the glacier snout well to the

north of the original passage. We were three days within it, three days in which optimism and pessimism alternatively held sway. It was not pleasant camping in the middle of the glacier tongue on a few square yards of doubtful sea ice with great, forbidding walls of ice towering above us on all sides. If one of those bergs rolled over while we were there, all our effort at Port Martin would be lost . . . and other things besides.

Here, in the glacier, we met the Emperor penguins again; no longer heading northward but all well fed, moving southwards towards the rookery. It was strange how we never saw them approaching, one minute we would be alone and the next we would have a group of Emperors regarding us with astonished interest. At our respective rates of progress we could be quite sure the Emperors would be home before we were.

The last day within the glacier tongue was the worst. We had been stopped by bad weather and a zone of weak ice ahead. The visibility was limited to a few yards but now and then in a lull in the driving snow we could vaguely see the blue walls of the surrounding icebergs towering above us. We slept, but by four a.m. were ready to move again when the visibility had eased to a hundred yards. We found that a fresh difficulty had arisen overnight. The passages among the icebergs, being narrow, had filled with deep, soft, unsettled snow which masked off all leads and weak ice. Worse still, when we attempted to advance, the weasels could not pull their heavily laden sledges in the deep snow.

We managed to go ahead very slowly, using two weasels roped together. These went forward about a hundred yards, ironing out a path. Then they returned along it to pull the sledges forward, one by one, over the road they had formed. Frequently the weasels would bog down in the bodiless snow, which meant that the men would have to worry them free before the advance could continue. This agonizingly slow progress would have been bad enough in fine weather but under the prevailing conditions of low temperatures and drifting snow it was exasperating. I was spared this heartbreaking labour, for my part was to walk ahead of the weasels with a shovel digging holes and sounding the ice for danger spots, leaving behind me at every hundred yards a marker consisting of a piece of red bunting on a bamboo stake to indicate the route. Here and there, the familiar red bunting would be replaced by a black one. This meant I had found a lead under the mantling snow and further delay for the weasel crew while they bridged it over with timber to work the weasels and sledges over, one by one. As for the route chosen, it was pure guesswork based on the logical enough theory that if we worked generally westward we must eventually emerge from the maze of icebergs.

Marret was showing the strain that he had been subjected to ever since we left Ile des Pétrels. It was no light matter to have the lives of us four dependent on his every decision. To have come so far and to lose at this final lap was his present fear. We could not help him, except to carry out his instructions, but every hour of the day one of us would be asking him to make some important decision. However, by six p.m. conditions had improved considerably. Then I found myself standing in a narrow passage between two bergs with a wide open field of sea ice opening out ahead and westward. Half a mile behind me the weasels had halted in the passage to camp the night. I hastened back to them with the happy news that we were through. Everyone was very tired and it was decided to move on only as far as the last berg where the ice was sounder than where they had halted. We did not consider it advisable to press any further with everyone as exhausted as they were. However, when the other three brought the weasels up to my furthest point, the sight of the open way to Ile des Pétrels was too much for them. Unanimously they reversed the decision and decided to push on. We had done no more than a further fifty yards when Vincent, driving Coccinelle, slewed over sideways as he broke through the ice. We were now well used to this sort of thing and it seemed no time before we had Hirondelle hitched to a towing cable and Coccinelle pulled clear.

At the navigation trap of Hirondelle, I set my astro compass on the direct course for Ile des Pétrels, sighted on the pale slip of the moon and we commenced to run down the last leg. Suddenly, revealed by the weasel headlights, I saw a suspicious dark line in the snow ahead. We halted to investigate. It proved to be a wide and sinister lead, all but completely camouflaged by a film of paper-thin ice blanketed with fresh snow. We used every stick of timber we carried to bridge this, even stripping the interior of the weasel cabin for sheets of three-ply to give more bearing surface on the weak edges. Even so; it looked doubtful. Marret drove Hirondelle across, gently as though driving over edges. The makeshift bridge gave under the weight. We who were watching called out a warning as one side of the lead collapsed, and Marret stabbed his foot on the accelerator and scrambled the weasel across as the bridge collapsed behind him. We had to build a fresh bridge for each weasel. But the worst was over with one weasel standing by on the far side to help.

This took us several hours, in which time the moon that had been guiding us home was lost in gathering clouds. However we were due to make radio contact with Ile des Pétrels, so we asked them to light a beacon on the hill and fire Very pistols to guide us in, which they agreed to do. It seemed strange after this last month of living in a world of four men and three weasels, that any other humans existed. We half doubted whether the promised lights would appear. I remember, at the time, being obsessed with a fear that they would not appear due ahead of us. This was my professional pride as a navigator in jeopardy. I had halted the weasels pointing homeward at the last sight of the moon. It would be embarrassing if the Very lights went up astern of us!

Exactly as scheduled a bright red star flowered low on the southern horizon, dead ahead of the weasels. For us that glowing light was the accolade of victory, after thirty-four days of endeavour. Our three weasels with their trains of sledges began to run down the last ten miles to home. Surely, this was the strangest convoy that ever broke the silence of the polar night.

A little later we were under the rock cliffs of Ile des Pétrels and Prévost and Rivolier, electric torches in their hands, came running across the sea ice to meet us. Everyone was shaking hands and trying to talk at once. With pride we showed them the five tons of stores we had dragged with us back from Port Martin. They touched the two new weasels to assure themselves of their reality.

'And what's more,' cried Marrat, the strain gone now, 'we have brought back the whole cellar of Port Martin!'

We went into the hut and were almost repulsed by its friendly warmth. We had forgotten what temperatures above freezing felt like. We found the hut transformed. In our absence the three remaining had worked miracles. Curtains of green canvas hung over the bunks, forms had been hacked out of solid oak bearers to replace the packing cases that served as chairs before. Rivolier had used our meagre supply of paint and his own artistic talents to good effect, transforming the very spirit of the hut with splashes of bright colour. But the crowning glory was in the south-western corner of the hut. Here they had built a miniature bar, complete with curved counter, a zinc top, and stool and footrest. We who had returned were touched by their efforts and sensibility in making a new atmosphere to match the mood of a triumphant conclusion to a hazardous enterprise. The table was covered with our best oilcloth and spread with the meal they had prepared to welcome us home. The hut, which had just been a warm and homely place before we left, was transformed into the magnificent place in the world.

How good it was to be back! And back we were, with the winter journey to Port Martin behind us. The howling of the dogs sounded like music to our ears as we drifted off to sleep in warm bunks.

6

The Rise of Fram

Now that the Port Martin project had been accomplished, the whole future of our group was transformed. No longer were we living from hand to mouth. We had ample food for the rest of the year, three weasels, full equipment for the dog teams, in fact everything that we needed to make us a normal expedition. The credit for this achievement must go to Marret. True, it was a team effort, and all members of the team, particularly Vincent, played their parts to the best of their abilities, but the concept and its execution were his. The driving force that kept the weasels rolling when conditions were at their worst sprang from Marret, alone. He was our leader.

But now we had a shortage of a leader of a different sort in our organization. Since Boss's defeat in battle and subsequent demoralization before we left, his team had had no leader. We had to find an exceptionally tough and intelligent dog to take over the wild, young team. The question was which? The problem in selecting a leader is that not only must he be intelligent, but he must also possess the fighting ability to control his team by fear. The two qualities do not necessarily go together.

Poor Boss was now a pitiable shadow of his former self. During our absence Paton had grown out of roly-poly puppyhood into a young dog. He had found in the broken-hearted leader a victim he could terrorize with impunity.

144

It was sad to see the scarred old victor of countless bloody battles cringing and grovelling before a half-grown dog like Paton, when Paton himself was not capable of holding his own against the weakest dog in the team Boss had ruled so short a while ago.

Within the team itself, anarchy was rife. Leaderless, the team of young dogs were continually brawling among themselves and had not been used for two months. Astro, the big white dog, held the leadership very shakily. It needed a stronger and wiser dog than he.

One rather significant thing had happened recently. Fram, the lazy sycophant of a lieutenant in Bjorn's team, had broken his chain and made a bloody tour of the dog lines, in which he attacked and beat every dog save one, his own leader Bjorn, with whom he still lived in a state of cringing fear.

This showed his ability as a fighter, and there was little doubt about his intelligence if a marked skill at avoiding work could be classed as such. Every one of us had had experience of Fram's sly cunning, when driving Bjorn's team. Every trace would be taut, but the sledge would not be advancing as it should. If a finger was hooked over Fram's trace he could be pulled back a yard before he realized his laziness had been detected. He could travel for miles with just enough strain on the trace to give the impression he was pulling. It was barely possible that in Fram we had the new leader we needed. Physically, he was a magnificent specimen; a big dog of about a hundred pounds with a deep chest and heavy thighs mounted on short, sturdy legs. His forehead was broad, and his eyes sharp and inquisitive. He was, of all our dogs, the most typical of the popular conception of a husky. For want of a better, Fram was to have his chance. Fram was to be moved to the young dogs' team to become its leader, and Maru, the philosophic penguin killer, from the young dogs to replace Fram in Bjorn's team.

This had only just been decided when Fram and his new team were called upon to do their first journey, without any previous training under their new leader. It happened thus. It was decided that a journey to the west would be made on the sea ice, with two weasels supported with a team of dogs. The object was to explore the coastline westward to the border of French Antarctic Territory. It was our major exploratory project. However the departure was delayed several weeks while food and equipment were prepared and the two weasels were overhauled for the journey. Practically on the eve of departure, I was making the routine pilot balloon observation from the top of the hill when I perceived a thin dark line on the northern horizon which suggested open water. Farther, the clouds to the north were black from the reflection of the water beneath, a phenomenon known as 'water-sky.' Coupled together these two indications made it almost certain that little sea ice remained. Marret decided to send a dog team north to confirm these suspicions. Rivolier and I went and as a team we took the youngsters under Fram.

We began by putting Fram in harness at the sledge alone and then bringing over the members of his team, one by one, for mutual introduction. This was accomplished much more speedily than we had anticipated, and done comparatively painlessly. A brief scrimmage ensued as each dog was attacked, beaten, then formally acknowledged his new leader by fawning and licking Fram's jaws. Astro, the big white dog, offered no resistance at all. He saw in Fram a much tougher proposition than he could hope to handle, so immediately acknowledged Fram's leadership in the approved fashion, and elected himself as Fram's lieutenant to aid Fram in subjugating the rest of the team. Pomme, the big Labrador, fell in for the worst treatment. Because he was completely different from the rest of the team, he was singled out for special attention. All the dogs delighted in attacking Pomme, and Fram was no exception. Pomme never made formal submission, no matter how decisively beaten he always whined back defiance. Perhaps Fram saw in this unquenchable defiance a future threat to his own supremacy, so he never wasted an opportunity to show Pomme who was master.

I apologized, in advance, to Rivolier for Fram. I had selected him and, though I hoped he would ultimately make a good leader, I did not expect he would be of much use immediately. We left in fine style. The main trouble was Fram's position in the team. Never before had he been on his own, out in front of a team; he was used to having Bjorn's tail waving just in front of him. So instead of going out to the end of his longer trace, he kept falling back to a subordinate position, in order to get a tail ahead of him. This, of course, did not help the driver to keep the team on course.

Just as bad was his lethargic way of life. One expects a leader to set an example to the rest of the team in eagerness to work, but with Fram, this first time, expectation was all there was. At every halt the first dog down on his belly was the leader, and when the command to mush was given, every dog would be on his feet, straining at his trace, except Fram who would still be slowly and reluctantly getting onto his feet, and only doing that through the threat of the driving whip and the imminent danger of being run down by the sledge which would be already under way. Continually, on the march, he kept glancing back, fearful that he might have missed a command to stop. However reluctant as he was to assume the responsibilities of his new office, he wasted no time in claiming its perquisites in the form of the attentions of the bitch, Helen. I felt that I had been prudent in apologizing to Rivolier about him before we left.

As we travelled I took stock of the team and felt confident that with further training we would have a good one in them. This was the hard core of the team, Fram the big leader, Astro who was now Fram's self-elected lieutenant, Seismo, the tough little egg, and finally Helen, who was the hardest and toughest traveller of them all, a compact little mass of bone and sinew, always straining at her trace. Each of these dogs had one virtue accentuated that set it a little above the normal run of dogs, and the four together merged into a single working unity. With Fram it was intelligence, with Astro brute strength, with Seismo it was dependability, and with Helen it was tireless endurance. The remainder were just dogs. There was Wild, tall and gangling, too fine in build ever to be a first-class dog; Roald, a coward in battle and as a result terrorized by the others; and finally Pomme, big, slow and clumsy though immensely powerful, horribly handicapped in this land of driving snow by his long woolly hair which could become a mass of ice in a matter of an hour of drift.

We camped that night at Ile Fram, a small rocky island some nine miles from base. We chose this early camp, partly because the weather was getting worse, but mainly because since the sea ice had broken out ahead of us, we did not wish to find ourselves forced to camp on floating ice near open water in a blizzard. There was a keen, cold wind carrying with it drift snow. It was a cold camp. In our haste to get away from camp in the morning we both assumed that the other had loaded the sponge rubber sleeping-mats on to the sledge. After mutual recriminations we made our bunks on bare ice. Though we were now past mid-winter the temperatures were still low enough to cause each of us to make a mental note that sleeping-mats were something more than ornaments in a tent!

That night we discussed our plans. Tomorrow we would leave as soon as it was light enough to travel. We estimated that the edge of the sea ice was about ten miles away, so with luck we could visit it and still return to Ile Fram the same day. Thus we would eliminate the risk involved in making a camp on the sea ice, which obviously was so unstable as to be likely to blow out in the first gale. Then, the reconnaissance made, we could count on being back at the hut on the third day.

So we planned it, but the elements deemed otherwise. The next morning dawned dull and overcast. It was one of those blank, featureless days when snow, ice and sky merge into one misty whole, leaving no shadow or relief, just a painful, white sameness. It was still very cold and a light drift was sweeping by. As it had improved slightly since the previous night, we considered it would not get any worse but would probably improve further so we broke camp. I always find it a cheerless business pulling down a camp on a day like this. It is the one point of warmth and comfort on this desolate ice plain and, instead of cherishing it, we pull it down. Our boots were frozen and tying up the sledge loads with bare hands was disagreeable. It was a relief to handle the ice-encrusted fur of the dogs, because as we worked them into their frozen harnesses, our fingers could detect a suspicion of warmth. We were glad to be under way, with our backs to the wind, and our exertions driving the blood through our veins.

We had been travelling some two hours when we admitted that the weather, far from improving, was getting worse. Visibility had imperceptibly closed in. The drift was thicker and the wind was rising rapidly. We turned and ran for Ile Fram. We had been travelling a further half-hour when it closed down completely and further travel became impossible. We did not know where we were or where we were heading. Only with difficulty could we make conversation. The dogs bunched together, each trying to shelter against his fellows, and refusing to drive head on to the wind.

Somehow, we managed to get the tent up. By the time we had the dogs staked out a full blizzard was upon us. Lacing up the tent, I saw the dogs, eight yards away, disappear in the swirling snow. The empty sledge was already half buried. We tied the funnel securely and crawled into our sleeping-bags. Once there, with our pipes alight we could discuss the situation.

Normally, when sledging over solid land, there would be nothing disquieting about such a situation. It was the fact that we were camped on ice, a yard or so thick, which gave food for thought. We estimated that we must be some fifteen miles from land and about five miles from the edge of open water. The last big blizzard had broken out a belt of sea ice over fifty miles wide to drive it out into the stormy wastes of the southern ocean, where it had been smashed to fragments in the havoc of the gales. As far as we could see, here we were with an excellent chance of following that ice, we and our tent on our own particular block. In the shrieking fury that was raging outside the thin fabric of the tent we would hear and know nothing, if our ice broke out. For all we knew, even as we talked we might well be already on our way northward, broken loose from land.

As Rivolier remarked, the thing that appealed to him most was that even if we did know, there was nothing we could do about it. To break camp and try to reach land in this weather was quite hopeless; the dogs could not drive, and we would have no idea where we were heading. So with a perfectly clear conscience he could compose himself for sleep.

The following day was, if anything, worse. I went out to feed the dogs and had difficulty in finding them though they were only eight yards away. They had curled up, backs to the wind and the blizzard had buried them, each snug in his hole in the snow protected from the lash of the wind. I found them by crawling round until the snow under me erupted as a head came up. I would push a cake of dog food into the open jaws, then the head would withdraw to eat in what passed for comfort for a husky. Having fed them I tried to find the sledge but it was either buried or blown away. The wind was howling insanely, the drift was as thick as a wall, and my face was a mask of ice. Finding the tent again took me a further ten minutes. It may sound ridiculous since all this searching was within a radius of ten yards, but such is a real Adélie Land blizzard.

To add to the enjoyment of the day, the washer on the filler cap of the primus gave up the ghost. That showed us a minor refinement in the discomfort of camping in the cold that we had not yet experienced. The intense cold had changed the soft, oiled washer into a substance resembling brittle bakelite, which had cracked into fragments. We tried many substitutes, packing with fabric greased with butter, a piece of leather carved out of a boot, and a washer off a petrol flask, with about the same degree of success with each, so that for the rest of the trip the lighting of the primus was introduced by an overture of blasphemous comment by the man lighting it. That would not have been so bad, but it also developed an alarming habit of bursting into flames once lighted. As a flaming primus is a source of considerable danger in the narrow confines of a tent this meant that every time that we wished to use the primus we had to have the funnel of the tent open, so that the primus could be thrown out if the flames got out of control. All this made life a little less enjoyable than strictly necessary.

It was during that first afternoon that we heard, even above the howl of the blizzard, a piercing cry.

'What the devil was that?' I asked Rivolier.

'Nothing, my dear Dovers, nothing at all. The cry of a sea bird, without doubt an albatross, one of the birds of the wide open ocean,' he replied. 'Which raises, however, an interesting academic question. Has the albatross flown in to see us, or have we made a voyage out to see the albatross?'

That night we made radio contact with the base. Neither Rivolier nor I were expert telegraphists. To us the radio was a rather unnecessary encumbrance in the tent. Neither of us expected to get much in the way of results from it, and were rarely disappointed. When occasionally we established contact, we tended to regard the apparatus with disbelief and suspect a trick somewhere. We had difficulty in deciphering their signal. We finally decided that their message was—

'Where are you?'

That seemed to be the question. We would have liked to know for sure, ourselves. We debated several suitable replies but finally replied with:

'We hope that we are still only four miles north of Ile Fram!' We agreed that this was a remarkable piece of telegraphic abbreviation, condensing, as it did, in one short sentence, all the hopes and fears that would be difficult to express in several paragraphs.

The second day closed with no change in the situation, and the third day of the blizzard was heralded by a miserable dawn. We found the tent interior about half the size it had been when we made camp, for the snow heaped up by the blizzard had pressed the walls inward. The howl of the wind did not sound so unbearable as before but we deduced, rightly, that this was only due to the tent being almost completely buried.

Snow is an excellent insulator. The heaped-up snow prevented the escape of warmth from the lighted primus and the rime on the tent walls melted and ran, only to freeze again as solid ice as soon as the primus was put out. The only way we could don our frozen boots was to heat them over the primus, and then get into them quickly, before they could freeze again. We had to tunnel our way out of the tent to feed the dogs, and found the same shrieking wind and driving snow as yesterday. Both the dogs and the sledges were completely buried. There was nothing to be seen outside, for the dense snow limited visibility to a few feet. We could be driving northward into the southern ocean on our floe or be still safely attached to land. It was with relief that we crawled back into the tent after the dogs' needs were cared for.

The ailing primus was a source of amusement all day. Once it was extinguished after cooking a midday meal, it took us the whole of the time to the next meal to get it going again. We had a small chess set and played several games to fill in the weary hours. We were playing either the championship of Terre Adélie, or that of the southern ocean, for we could not decide which; we would have to wait until the blizzard stopped to decide. Most of the time we slept.

Towards four in the morning we woke to a deathly silence. The drumming fabric of the tent was still, and the high whine of the wind had ceased. The blizzard had so obsessed our minds for the last three days that it was difficult to believe that it was at last over. Now, we would be able to see, and know the answer to the question that had been worrying us. Outside the tent it was flat calm, the dogs had crawled out of the snow in which they had sheltered and were shaking themselves clear of accumulated snow. Fram growled at Astro who wriggled on his belly to Fram, licking his chops in formal submission. The handlebars of the sledge were all there was of it above the snow, and looking over them we could see, away to the south, a low-lying dark mass which could only be Ile Fram. The blizzard had done its worst but we were still connected to land by unbroken sea ice.

There were several hours of hard work digging the tent and sledge out of the snow. Leaving Rivolier to finish this, I took the empty sledge and five of the dogs to visit a berg about a mile away, in order to climb it and see what could be seen from a height of two hundred feet. I halted the sledge at the foot of the berg and began climbing its icy wall. The dogs decided to follow me with the sledge, but, after a few minutes of scrambling ineffectively against the sheer face of ice, they gave up and followed Fram's example, who was sitting down awaiting developments.

Climbing up the face of the berg was slow work. The slope was too steep to negotiate with crampons alone and I had to cut steps and handholds with my ice-axe. The ice was incredibly brittle in the cold. The point of the ice-axe hit like an explosive bullet, dislodging masses of ice which were impossibly large compared with the force of the blow that dislodged them. I had the impression that if I hit a little harder the whole mass of the iceberg would disintegrate. Several times a fall of ice nearly swept me off the face of the berg. The pieces broken out went skittering down, making tinkling sounds, and as they caught the sunlight, they looked like a shower of sapphires. The dogs, being immediately below me, were under constant bombardment, and a yelp from Fram advertised that his slumbers had been rudely interrupted. He promptly attacked Astro in reprisal, rather to Astro's astonishment.

Once I had gained the top, my horizon was extended by ten miles and I had a magnificent view. To the south the sea ice stretched unbroken to the land but to the north, I could see a long, black line of open water, running east-west, and turning in to meet the land near Pointe Eba. I thought of Marret, Vincent and Prévost who had camped in the weasel off Pointe Eba earlier in the year, for where they had camped was now the ocean. Now all we had to do to carry out our assignment was to travel to Pointe Eba to verify the exact conditions prevailing there.

My descent was more hurried than my ascent. About the sledge dog fighting had become general. Fram and Astro were attacking Roald, and the other two, excited by the sight and smell of blood, had joined in, sinking their fangs into whatever opportunity offered. As I had no wish to see Roald torn to pieces, I wasted no time in joining them, doing the last forty feet in an involuntary slide, arriving among the dogs amid a cascade of falling ice. The dogs must have thought that the avenging angel had descended upon them.

Fram, the originator of the mischief, saw me coming and with his customary acumen withdrew from the massacre as far as his trace would permit him, to sit, a picture of saintly innocence, which was however slightly spoilt by the blood dripping from his jaws. Astro, Wild and Helen were soon dispersed with a few cracks of the whip, but Seismo had to be dragged bodily off the screaming Roald. I gave him a sound beating, but the moment I turned my back on him to deal with the other culprits a howl of anguish from Roald announced that Seismo had returned to the attack.

Fram watched the whole proceedings like an uncertain seraph, his tail wagging apologetically, but his expression slowly changed and his nervousness became more acute as I moved towards him, and it changed to panic as he divined my intention.

A little later a rather subdued team dragged the sledge back to where Rivolier awaited us at the old camp site with the gear ready packed for the next move forward. Fram, for the first time, slipped naturally into his place as leader and at each command his response was quick and accurate.

It was a clear, cold day, the surface was good and the sledge ran easily, its runners whispering as they slid over the crisp snow. It was good to be travelling except where, here and there, we struck zones of soft, brashy snow, similar to those which had so plagued the weasels on the return to Port Martin. In these the dogs sank to their bellies, the sledge ploughed deep, while we floundered along laboriously, sinking to our thighs. But for the greater part of the day we were half running to keep up with the sledge.

The first intimation we had that we were nearing the edge of the ice were a series of narrow leads, yard-wide ribbons of black water cutting across the sledge route. A little later we found ourselves engaged in a chaos of rafted floes. There was little need to push on farther, for this field of shattered ice was the result of the wild sea pounding on the edge of the ice. The sea itself could not be far away. Rivolier stayed with the sledge and I walked on alone over the last five hundred yards, jumping from loose floe to loose floe.

Here was the ocean; no mere lake among the floes, this, but the unbounded sea, stretching away to the northward, dark, sinister and unrelieved by even the smallest ice floe. One could set sail from here and bring up to Australia. Towards the west the ice edge turned south to join the continent at Pointe Eba. Apparently, the only sea ice remaining on the Adélie Land coast was the comparatively small section over which we had just travelled. Everywhere else the ice had gone with the gales. Our weasel track to the west over the frozen sea was blocked. No road lay here. Where we had driven with the weasels, coming back from Port Martin, was open water. We had only just gone back in time.

Out of the black water, a seal rose and blew, and his breath hung in the air like a dense puff of smoke, while some distance away I could see a group of Emperor penguins sporting in the water. For them the loss of the sea ice was no tragedy; instead of a hundred miles of walking over the ice to food, they only had to come this far to fish.

This was the ocean, dark and menacing, and the yard thick floes on which I stood seemed paper thin. I thought of the open leads which lay between us and good, firm land. I wasted little time in rejoining Rivolier and the dogs.

This time there was no question of a second camp out on the floes. We had a hasty meal standing by the sledge, stamping about to keep ourselves warm. The dogs crowded about, tails wagging, hoping for a morsel of our food. As we intended to drive non-stop until we reached Ile Fram, we shared our repast with them. Each dog was given one biscuit and a small piece of pemmican which he seized and gulped down. Handing out biscuits to that hungry group was a dangerous business. We narrowly missed adding a hand or two to their ration. The only exception was Fram. I would not say we had to force his biscuit upon him but he took it so disdainfully, that he seemed to be conferring an honour upon the giver in accepting it. This was another indication of the change of character that was taking place in this erstwhile cringing, lazy dog.

The next came when we commenced the long, cold run back to Ile Fram. A wind had sprung up, a light drift was blowing, and our course kept us headed into it. Fram seemed to have sensed our intentions, for without a command given, he maintained a steady course for Ile Fram. He was beginning to understand his responsibilities as a leader.

I broke through into the water while crossing a lead and my wet clothing was covered with ice when I got out. My trouser legs were like stove pipes and I had to keep moving to keep them flexible. It was dark and I felt miserable when we finally pulled to a halt under the black rocks of Ile Fram. While Rivolier arranged the tent, ran out the wireless aerial, and began cooking a meal, I staked out the tired dogs. There was not much energy left in any of them; the happy-hearted brawlers of twelve hours ago were only interested in their lump of pemmican and sleep. All that is, except the indestructible Helen. In all my experience of the team, I never once saw that little, black-hearted she-devil show signs of fatigue. Even now she was nosing the dogs on either side of her, trying to stir up trouble. As I tied each dog, he rubbed his ice-covered muzzle between my legs to free his frozen eyes and jaws. Fram, I decided to leave loose. Partly to show him a leader had privileges, and partly because he was a veteran escapologist anyway. It was reasonably safe too, because he had become violently attached to Helen and showed no inclination to move more than a few yards from her. Helen did not seem to return his affection to the same degree; if anything, she showed a preference for Astro, his lieutenant. The moment Fram turned his back on her she would be rubbing noses with Astro, or with some other member of the team. Fram soon discovered that he could not afford to be more than a yard off her tail. So we found that to chain Helen was automatically to tie up Fram.

The next day a half-blizzard was blowing. We stayed in camp, for there was no need to hurry back to base. The western journey would have to be completely replanned, now that the route over the sea ice was gone. We were not bored. The damaged primus saw to that. It kept us amused the whole day as we struggled with it to produce some warm food. When we emerged from the tent we found that Fram had rounded up a passing Emperor penguin during the night and had the unfortunate bird at bay against the tent. This was a demonstration of another trait in Fram's character. With any other of our dogs, we would have found only a few feathers and bloodstains if they had had Fram's opportunity with that penguin. Anything weaker than themselves, they killed. Fram was an exception; he never killed wantonly. In fact, it could be said he never killed, even in necessity. I tried to take him with me for a walk around the island, and though he fawned about me, eager to be caressed, he only followed me for fifty yards before he began looking back at the team, *his* team, and after a few more yards had deserted me to bound back to them and to Helen.

The following day we could just see the pale disc of the sun showing weakly through the drifting snow. This was all we needed to steer a course for the base, and within twenty minutes from the time the sun broke through we had the sledge packed and we were under way, with Fram and the team pulling like veterans.

On returning we found that Marret had revised his plans for the western journey. Instead of travelling on the sea ice, we would go over the plateau with both weasels and dogs.

As weather conditions on the plateau would be too difficult until late October, the trip was tentatively planned to commence on the first of November. Meanwhile Rivolier and I would begin a study of the sea ice in the hope that we could find a solution to several problems that had troubled us during the return from Port Martin.

To do this we began a detailed study of what ice remained in the bay. We suspected that the zones of weak ice that we had encountered resulted from undulations in the surface of the sea ice due to pressure, so that areas forced below the level of the water deteriorated. In any case, we realized that the formation and ultimate breaking out of the sea ice left a large gap, of which we knew relatively little. On the Port Martin journey, in discussing the time and effort wasted digging holes through the snow to check the ice beneath, we had talked vaguely about detecting weakness in the ice by electrical means. These zones of weakness had always been associated with salt water flooded ice. The electrical conductivity of sea water is high, while that of dry snow is almost nil. If a probe was designed which could be forced into the snow, and was capable of indicating the conductivity of the layers it passed through, then we could dispense with digging holes. Marret was never happier than when tinkering with a new idea and making some new equipment. He went to work with a soldering iron and lengths of wire.

Previously, Rivolier had asked him if he could design an automatic recorder to register the relative intensity of sunshine in the winter months, so that he could use the results in his study of the reactions of animal life to Antarctic conditions. In due time the apparatus was produced. It consisted, briefly, of two plates of metal, the one polished and the other blackened. Its operation depended on their different rates of absorption of radiant energy. On trials, due to minor technical difficulties, it failed to do the work for which it was planned. However, we found that with it we could detect the direction of the hot stove from any corner of the hut.

Since I was the chief hole-digger of the Port Martin trip Marret took me with him when he made the first trial of the new ice detector. He was bubbling over with enthusiasm, quite certain of success. I was still sceptical. I remembered the sunshine recorder. He plunged the probes of his gadget into a layer of heavy snow. The needle of the dial registered changes of current as the probes penetrated. Suddenly, it swung off the dial completely.

'Water and rotten ice at sixty-five centimetres,' announced Marret. I dug down with a shovel and found what he had diagnosed, much to my surprise, and, I suspect, also to his. Like a pair of children with a new toy, we raced around the bay, making fresh trials. Each time the detector gave us an accurate picture of what lay beneath the mantling snow. We had moved out of the era of the shovel. Elated, we brought each of the others to see the detector at work.

It was with this detector and more direct means that Rivolier and I began our examination of the sea ice. Marret gave us a weasel as transport, since the main part of our work consisted of laying out a line of stakes as far to seaward as we could and taking a series of measurements at each. The weasel was an excellent idea. In it we had our apparatus, our sleeping gear, and all the food we needed; we were a self-contained unit. If caught out on the sea ice in bad weather, all we had to do to make camp was to shut the weasel door and camp in the cabin.

The first day we headed north with the idea of doing the work away from land first. About three miles out we encountered an open lead camouflaged by a scum of fresh snow. It was ten feet wide and the skin of snow and ice masking the water was only a few inches thick. The first indication we had of its existence was when the weasel lurched. The snow under the tracks fragmented and only the speed of the machine carried it to the other side, where the tracks engaged just sufficiently to scramble the machine out amidst a welter of breaking ice. This lead was to assume great importance to us in the next weeks and we called it the 'big lead.'

We had crossed it by jumping it at top speed, a process which occasionally works, but one that is not recommended. Not, that is, for anyone desiring an uneventful life as we were. We decided that we would not attempt to repeat the manœuvre on the way back but would bridge it with timbers. Having marked the lead with a marker flag, we went on.

'You know,' I remarked to Rivolier, who was driving, 'it's practically certain that we will break through shortly, if your last effort was anything to go by.'

Whereupon, before he had time to reply, the weasel gave a sidewise lurch and shuddered to a halt, bow down. Water flooded over the tracks. We had done it again. The danger, of course, was only to the machine, in that unless it was extricated quickly the water, no longer insulated from the cold air, would freeze, thus making the weasel an integral part of the local scenery that nothing short of dynamite could break out. And dynamite exploded under the hull was not calculated to do the weasel much good.

We tried all the normal tricks learnt by bitter experience on the Port Martin journey to work it out of the brash, without any marked degree of success, until, finally, we managed to work a plank under the tracks and in reverse with the tracks gripping on the plank, the machine backed out.

'At least,' remarked Rivolier, 'that's one way of finding a zone of weakness for our study.'

After several hours of work, placing our stakes with our backs towards land, the weather began to look threatening, and looking back we could see the plateau becoming indistinct under a haze of drifting snow that betokened an oncoming blizzard. Accordingly, we called it a day and began the retreat to camp. Between us and land still lay the big lead that we had jumped and which required bridging. It so happened that on our side of the lead a set of heavy bridging had been spotted in case it might be needed on the now cancelled western coastal journey. These we decided, being more solid than the normal timbers carried for this purpose, would be ideal. Particularly so since we wanted to leave them in position as a bridge over the lead permanently, for we would have to cross the lead many times in the future to continue our work. We estimated that we would have sufficient time before the blizzard was upon us to find the timbers, drag them to the lead, build a bridge and then return to camp.

That estimate was over-optimistic. By the time we had found and dug them out the weather was getting difficult. The drift was becoming intense and the wind was rising alarmingly. We succeeded in attaching the bridging to the weasel and got under way. Before we could locate the lead, the blizzard had closed down on us. Visibility was only three yards and the wind was over sixty knots. As we could not afford to go blundering on blindly in search of the big lead, lest we find it in an uncomfortable manner, we did the only thing possible and halted the machine, closing the doors, and settling down to camp in the cabin.

Once more we had been caught on the sea ice. The position was similar to our last camp on the sea ice with the dogs in a blizzard. This time, between us and land was a wide-open lead, dividing the sea ice in the bay in two sections. If the sea ice were to continue to break out, the logical point of division was that lead. All ice to the south would stay attached to land, and all in the north, including that on which we were camped, would be blown out to sea to disintegrate in the gales. We would have been so very much happier had we been but a few hundred yards south of our present position on the safe side of the lead. But in our present case, as it had been with the dogs previously, there was nothing we could do about it; to drive on blindly in the tempest would just be asking for trouble.

So we settled down in our sleeping-bags to sit out the blizzard patiently, feeling that, once more, the *petit bonhomme du plateau* was making sport of us.

We had in the library at the hut the book describing the raft journey across the Pacific of the Kon Tiki Expedition, and we both had read it several times, for it described so marked a difference in life to that which we were living as to form a real escape from ice and cold. We discussed the possibility of making a second and involuntary Kon Tiki Expedition in our weasel. We both agreed that the possibilities seemed excellent. It was difficult, however, to imagine our clumsy vehicle afloat, for although by design they are amphibious, they are not that amphibious, for they float with only a few inches of freeboard. I amused myself in deciding what could be done to make the weasel more seaworthy. This seemed to call for stripping out the engine and every bit of equipment to make the machine a light shell.

Rivolier, on the other hand, was not interested in my musings; he could see a brief and definite solution to my problems. He spent the day trying to decide of what the weasel reminded him. I suggested a prison cell but there were no bars. We had a ham hanging in the weasel as part of our food supply, and this, coupled with the general aura of untidiness suggested an old farm cart on its way to market to him. Nothing in our surroundings suggested a modern motor vehicle.

When we closed down as the blizzard struck, we still had the heavy bridging timbers attached to the weasel, and the last thing we had done before shutting the cabin door was to plant a line of marker flags for fifty yards ahead of the weasel. To avoid being buried by the dense snow carried by the wind we could advance the weasel a few yards every two hours, and the marker flags would guide us over safe ground. But we had under-estimated the speed with which the machine was being buried. At our first attempt to drive the machine forward, we heard a rendering crash even above the howl of the wind. The tow line to the already buried bridging timbers had parted. The weasel pointed its nose almost vertically. For a moment I thought that the ice had broken under us but the machine clambered out of the prison the snow had built about us and once more sat on an even keel. As for the marker flags, the drift was so intense that a hand held twelve inches from one's face was invisible, so we saw nothing of them. All we could do was to flounder a few yards ahead each time, hoping that the next advance would not bring us into the open lead.

There was a wearying sameness in this travel by weasel on the sea ice. Sitting in the weasel cabin, listening to the scream of the wind, and being jolted as the weasel shuddered under the gusts, all this seemed to have become a normal part of our life. Since our visit to the edge of the ice, we neither of us had any illusions about its stability. Each of us many times remarked to the other, 'If we were only on the landward side of the lead we would not have a thing to worry us.'

We both decided that in the future, if a future was granted to us, we would never again camp to seaward of the lead. Whatever happened we would cross the lead and camp on ice that was firmly attached to land. Another day came and went, with day and night merging imperceptibly into one. We chatted away through the waking hours between meals and the rest of the time we curled up in our sleeping-bags and slept.

When the weather let up, we found we could not get the engine to start. The best we could manage was to squeeze a few reluctant coughs from the machine. We persevered for quite some time but failed to locate the source of the trouble. There was only one thing to do, much as it hurt our pride. We radioed the base for assistance and the expert Vincent.

Vincent and Marret were with us in a very short lapse of time, driving Coccinelle, the second weasel. It was good to know that the 'big lead' had not widened. They smiled the knowing smiles of professionals as we explained what we thought was wrong and what measures we had taken to rectify the trouble. Out of politeness, they made a show of listening, but we could see that they were not bothering to hear us, already they were deciding what should be done.

Our pride in ourselves as amateur mechanics was salved as they tried one thing after another without success. We began to discuss whether we should all camp there together for the night. While Vincent delved in the innards of Hirondelle, we used Coccinelle to tow the bridging timbers to the lead, where, with them, we built a permanent bridge. All was ready for our return to base except Hirondelle.

'You know,' remarked Rivolier, apropos of nothing, 'when I was a child we used to amuse ourselves by putting a potato over the exhaust of motor-cars. The car won't start then.'

After Vincent had dismantled the exhaust tube and melted out a foot of solid ice, formed by drift snow blowing into the exhaust and solidifying, Hirondelle started with the first touch on the self-starter. We then returned in convoy to the base.

The next day found Rivolier and I away bright and early on the sea ice, putting in our stakes and taking our measurements. But before night closed down we retreated from the seaward side of the lead, crossed the bridge and camped a hundred yards on the landward side of the lead. As we ate our evening meal in the weasel cabin, we remarked how comforting it was to be camped on sea ice on the safe side of the big lead. Let the blizzard blow, we had little to worry about. We could see our future work being done speedily and in comfort. We could camp in the middle of our zone of operations in this safe camp, and with the bridge in permanence, could cross the lead as we wished, and be always sure of returning to this camp. Being self-contained in the weasel, we had no need to return to the base each night and thus would be able to get an early start each morning and so waste none of the rare periods of fine weather.

At noon the following day, we had a visit from shore, when Prévost, Duhamel and Lépineux came out with a dog team. They had sighted five seals at the crack near a grounded iceberg and were on their way to hunt them for dog food. After a few words of greeting, with a crack of the whip, they left us and were speeding towards the seals. About four p.m. Rivolier drew my attention to vast spirals of blizzard on the plateau. It was apparent that within less than an hour a fresh blizzard would be upon us, so we stopped work and retreated to our safe camp near the bridge over the lead. We were about to settle down for the night there, when we noticed the dog team over near the glacier, still dressing the seals that they had killed. It was obvious to us that from where they were, sheltered by the glacier, they could not see the angry claws of the oncoming blizzard reaching over the plateau towards them. So we decided to drive over and warn them, and having gone so far, that we might just as well return to the base for the night. Accordingly, we hitched our sledge barge containing all our stores and equipment and drove in towards Ile des Pétrels where we dumped the barge about fifty yards from shore, where it would be ready to use the next day, and drove over to the seal hunters.

As soon as we warned them of the impending blizzard, Prévost and Duhamel turned the dogs and raced shorewards with them to the shelter of the hut. There were four seal carcasses on the ice so Lépineux elected to stay with us to help in towing them back to the base with the weasel. By the time we had the carcasses attached on towing cables and were ready to leave, the blizzard was upon us; not yet in full fury, but the wind was very strong and the drift snow was becoming thicker. This did not worry us greatly, we were still on sea ice but were very close to land and well on the safe side of the lead. We would, of course, try to get back to the hut, but if conditions became too difficult, we would just stop the weasel, close the doors and camp the night wherever we happened to be. Only Georges Lépineux was at all concerned. He had his radio schedule to make that night, and he was a meticulously conscientious man in his duties. But for him, we would not have persevered, for by the time we reached the hut it had begun to blow in earnest.

We had intended to go out again the next day, but the blizzard intensified and it was impossible to leave the hut. The following day we woke to find that the blizzard had died off overnight and only a strong wind was blowing. Rivolier and I were getting our gear together, ready to clamber into the weasel and head northward over the sea ice again when Prévost burst into the hut.

'All the sea ice is gone!' he cried. 'The open sea is washing the shore of Ile des Pétrels!'

In next to no time, Rivolier and I were scrambling among the rocks towards the tops of the hill to verify this astounding news. We could not help feeling that Prévost was joking.

He was not!

We had very little to say to each other as we gazed northward. All the sea ice had gone, all except a narrow strip connecting Ile des Pétrels with Pointe Géologie. The white expanse to which we had become so accustomed was gone. Not a vestige of it remained, not even a floe a yard wide. In its place was the bare ocean, black, sullen and menacing. There was no point in looking for our bridge over the lead and our 'safe' camp beside it. That and all the ice between it and land had vanished overnight, and now was pounding to fragments among the storm-riven floes hundreds of miles to the north. Where once we had been camped with the dog team was open water, even our barge containing our supplies and instruments was gone, and both of us, in a manner of speaking, would have staked our lives on that being safe.

Quite silent, and full of sober reflections, the two of us tramped back to the hut. Without a word Rivolier took a bottle of cognac from the shelf and poured out two generous glasses. Still without a word, we each drained our glass.

Marret came into the hut, shaking his head, after inspecting the scene.

'If you had camped out there the other night,' he said, 'what a terrible blow it would have been for us this morning, when we went out to look for your camp!'

Rivolier and I nodded assent, but we were thinking of two other persons who would be undergoing an even more marked shock about this time, if we had not already begun to feed the euphausia on the ocean floor.

We thought of those five seals who by coming on to the ice at that critical moment had saved us from a watery grave.

'You know,' remarked Rivolier, 'whenever I go for a walk, I am going to carry a pocket full of sugar. Just in case I meet a seal.'

7

Helen and Others

The weeks that followed were lazy ones. For with the route westward over the sea ice no longer in existence, and it being too early in the season to go west on the plateau, we contented ourselves with the minor tasks of the little station. Fram and his team came under special attention and every possible day they were taken out with their sledge loaded with rocks for training. Firstly, it was individual training for Fram and Astro his lieutenant. Then as the desired improvement was achieved, another dog was added to the training group, until finally we had the whole team working together as a single unit under Fram's leadership.

Fram was a complex character, and with each day of his new position, he emerged more and more as a distinct individual. With his team he was all authority, bullying, punishing and meeting the least infringement with swift attack and slashing jaws, but with me, his driver, he was the same fawning, good-natured buffoon that we had known so well in the days before his sudden rise to power. Whereas all the other dogs were trained to stand still when being harnessed, and were corrected with a sharp cuff across the muzzle if they dared to move, Fram insisted on his privileges as a clown. After fawning all over me as I tried to harness him, he would bring me to the point of desperation by rolling over on his back, foolishly waving his paws in the air, with his harness only half on.

These were the two sides of the dog, the stern leader with his team and the friendly fool with his driver, but there were still others. He was possessed of a tremendous natural dignity that was unassailable by a mere man; one could get so close to Fram but no closer. He was prepared to be accepted as a friend and partner, but not as a pet. Every attempt I made, and I made many, to make a pet of him was met with a cold aloofness.

Fram knew almost precisely what I would tolerate in the way of minor misdemeanours. When he saw that his clowning was beginning to annoy me he would cease and become once more the perfectly behaved leader. I felt that while I was studying him very closely, he was studying me just as closely. Certainly he was insidiously putting me in my place as far as the rest of his team were concerned, and by gradually extending his authority he was outlining to me what he considered was his affair, and what he counted as mine. And once he decided on a course of action he had an amiable obstinacy of purpose that I found impossible to combat.

The behaviour of the team when we went seal-hunting was a case in point. I had established strict rules for the conduct of the teams while the driver was skinning the carcass. Stern discipline was always necessary, for the sight and smell of fresh blood excited the dogs' ravenous appetites, and unless the driver kept them under complete control there would be a sudden stampede and the dogs would be all over the seal. Therefore, when the team was about fifty yards from the catch they would be halted, and the driver would go ahead on foot to dispatch the animal. When the blubber had been stripped off in two flitches the driver would call the dogs, who would drag up the sledge and sit nearby in a half circle, tongues hanging out, watching each slash of the knife with avid interest. From time to time I would throw each dog in turn a chunk of meat, for it was too much to expect them to contain themselves a few yards from so much food.

Now, since open water had brought the seals back to us, and since our stock of seal meat was exhausted, it became urgent to kill as many seals as possible to be sure of food for the teams. As Fram's team was in training, they were used for hunting and for transporting the seals back to camp. I commenced the usual procedure at a kill.

Fram did not agree. The first revolt occurred when I shot the seal. He decided there was no point in waiting for my call, the gunshot was sufficient advice that there was now no chance of frightening the seal. So, as soon as the shot rang out, he brought the sledge up. His gang of young toughs, encouraged, came rushing in with their jaws agape. I was preparing to withstand boarders, when there was a sudden flurry and about turn by Fram and a few quick snaps. Then I found the team sitting in the usual half-circle facing Fram, who had planted himself between them and the seal. I offered the big dog a chunk of seal meat by way of reward, but he spurned it, leaving it untouched where it had fallen. He then got up and made a close inspection of the seal. Selecting a choice piece he tore it off and gulped it down, watching my reactions closely as he did so. At the same time, the other dogs had been all eyeing the first morsel that I had thrown to Fram. It became too much for them and there was a concerted rush. Fram's lazy insolence dropped away and he sprang into action. Immediately, the team recoiled into a half-circle with Fram watching over them growling.

A little later, I tried to give each a piece of seal, as was my usual custom. Fram objected strongly, falling on each dog as the meat was thrown to it, so that the meat lay where it had fallen, with the dog cringing on his belly to Fram. This was too much! The time had come for me to assert my waning authority. I took the whip off the sledge and advanced on Fram. He cringed a little to take the punishment, and as the whip fell, the dog in front of Fram took advantage of the diversion to edge towards his piece of meat. Even as

the whip fell, a deep-throated growl from Fram stopped the
dog, which whined in submission and remained still. Fram
was determined not to surrender his opinion, so for the rest
of the day he received beating after beating, in exactly the
same spirit, submissively but still exercising his authority
over the team. Not one of those dogs ate a morsel. I had to
confess in the end that I was beaten, and Fram, no doubt,
considered the training of his man was progressing satis-
factorily.

And this was the thin edge of a very long wedge. One by
one, Fram won point after point in a similar manner, and
once his point was gained, it was for all time. I was gradually
made to feel that I was a very minor piece of the equipment
of the sledge, barely necessary in fact; all I had to do was to
leave the management of the sledge and team entirely to
him, and content myself with issuing my purely formal orders. Of course all this did not happen at once, Fram was
too clever for that, but by the end of the year I felt that if I
were driving the team much longer, I would find myself the
possessor of a first-rate inferiority complex.

I think that Fram was at his most insolent the day that
Rivolier and I decided to take some measurements along a
new line of stakes placed on the sea ice that had reformed
after the last big blizzard. This new ice was too thin to sup-
port a weasel and the work had to be done on foot. We took
Fram along with us towing a light sledge on which was all
our paraphernalia. We would move from one flag to the next,
a distance of two hundred yards, where we would halt Fram
and his sledge while we took samples of the sea ice and
other measures, involving a stop of half an hour. Fram very
soon knew what was required of him. He would flop down
alongside the flag and watch our doings with the utmost of
contempt. When we had finished, we could call 'Mush!' to
Fram, and the big dog would just yawn in our faces. So we
would stride off, leaving him lying there. When we were

almost to the next flag Fram would get wearily to his feet, shrug his shoulders and bound after us, so that by the time we had reached the flag he would be already there, yawning with boredom.

There was one matter that did not bore Fram. That was Bjorn, his former leader. Until recently, Bjorn had been secure in his position of king dog, the undisputed master in battle of every dog in the lines, but since Fram's promotion, Fram had demonstrated that he too could handle any dog, so that the only remaining combat for kingship rested between Bjorn and Fram themselves. It was inevitable that this battle must take place, for there must always be a king dog. But neither Bjorn nor Fram showed any great inclination to force the issue, Fram because he had just emerged from two years as Bjorn's vassal, and Bjorn because he sensed the change that had taken place in his one-time cringing lieutenant.

We, the men, waited daily for the final clash. We never attempted to cause a battle, but, equally, never attempted to prevent the struggle from taking place. Either action by us would have been unfair. The two claimants seemed to be biding their time for a favourable opportunity to launch a decisive attack. On one side was Bjorn, the old champion, a very big and immensely powerful dog, skilled in battle but otherwise dull of intellect, while on the other side was Fram, the challenger, smaller and stockier, not so battle-wise, but highly intelligent. It was difficult to estimate who would be the victor; it was intelligence verses brute strength, and either could win.

If Bjorn had forced the issue when Fram first became a leader, there would have been no doubt about the outcome. The long years that Fram had spent in submission to Bjorn would have won the day for Bjorn. But Bjorn was uncertain, and hesitated. Thus, in hesitating, he gave Fram confidence, while the wily Fram avoided battle and undermined Bjorn's bullying self-assurance. It was two months before the issue was settled, two long months in which the two dogs made stiff legs at each other, growling defiance, or, as at times, studiously ignored the existence of each other. But over the whole period, for both men and the other dogs, the impending struggle added a sense of drama to the ordinary routine of polar life.

Helen, the devilish little bitch of Fram's team, was once more an expectant mother, and though Helen had never succeeded in raising a pup we were hoping to save this litter. They had been sired by Astro and should be well worth raising.

However, when we found her in the morning, the pups had been born four hours previously and all were dead, save one, a little black replica of its mother. A few hours later this last pup, too, was dead. Helen showed no feeling at all and leapt at the chain as I took her back to the dog lines. She took up her usual place between Fram and Astro, rubbed noses with the two dogs and was happy. The same afternoon she was out with the team, showing no sign that anything had happened.

All the dogs were classified as to their potential danger to the Emperor rookery. Maru and Helen each held a three-star rating. Either were capable of a large-scale massacre in the minimum of time. A few days later I had been for a run on the new ice with Fram's team, and having left the team to climb a rocky island, was horrified to see, on returning, an empty harness among the dogs. A little black dot disappearing in the direction of the Emperor penguin rookery was all I could see of Helen. Realizing it was quite hopeless to try to catch her, I jumped aboard the sledge and returned at a full gallop to the hut.

Everyone was inside the hut when I burst in, all in various corners quietly doing their own particular work.

'Helen is loose!'

The effect was electrical. Men immediately abandoned whatever they were doing, grabbing rifles, pistols or any armament available. There was no need for explanation, there was only one object in the exercise, to stop Helen from playing havoc among the Emperors.

Marret and Rivolier went direct to the rookery, Prévost round the back of Ile Rostard and the rest of us spread out to strategic posts about the island.

'Please don't shoot to kill unless you must,' I asked weakly. 'She's a very good sledge dog.'

But the air of determination about all the group made things look bad for Helen as well as for the Emperors.

Helen arrived almost simultaneously with the rookery group. She ran into Marret who opened fire, so swinging away she avoided him to disappear into the rookery. However in her blood lust as she fell on the nearest Emperors she did not notice Rivolier, so the first intimation she had of his presence were his bullets kicking up the snow about her. Deciding the operation was becoming difficult, she abandoned her victims and fled out of the rookery, dodging Marret to vanish behind Ile Rostard with shots hurrying her departure.

Ten minutes later Prévost, at the other entrance to the rookery on the opposite side of Ile Rostard, sprang into action as she came at a wolf trot, belly low to the ground, jaws agape, towards the penguins. As soon as Helen saw this line of attack was guarded she wheeled and disappeared.

An uneasy lull followed. The first attacks had been repelled with only a small loss of life, but now the little black fiend had vanished and unless we caught or killed her we would be in a state of perpetual alert.

A shout from Lépineux on the other side of the island sent Duhamel racing down the cliff out of my sight. I turned and ran back along the cliff leading back to camp and the penguins, ramming a cartridge home in the Mauser, ready to cover the unguarded side of Ile des Pétrels. Two quick shots from Duhamel failed to swerve her from her purpose as she ran past him, belly to the ground in the disturbed ice about the tide crack.

She came into my view at about 200 yards, rapidly drawing away. I opened fire, trying to drop the heavy bullets in front of her in order to turn her. At that range, however it was a chancy business with such a fast moving target. At each shot I held my breath, half afraid to see Helen drop in a lifeless heap. The bullets from the big rifle threw up a fountain of ice chips at each impact, but their only effect on Helen was to make her swerve a little away from the island.

As she turned at Rostard towards the rookery she would soon be out of my sight and I was obliged to change my tactics. Not knowing what the state of defence there was, in desperation I was obliged to line my sights on Helen and try to kill her, hoping that I would with luck only succeed in wounding her.

But the range was too long and the target moving too fast. She disappeared behind Rostard. A salvo of shots announced that the last line of defence was still holding, and Helen came back into view, running very fast, heading towards Pointe Géologie.

The second attack had been beaten off with no casualties to either side. What frightened us most was the fixity of Helen's purpose. She seemed to be completely obsessed with the Emperor penguins.

The position was getting desperate. We had visions of Helen establishing herself out on the ice, far from our reach, then at intervals descending on the penguins under cover of darkness or bad weather.

However, watching her out on the sea ice, she seemed to have become uncertain, running a few hundred yards, then stopping to look back. Perhaps she had had enough excite-

ment for one day, and would let herself be captured. I
walked out on the sea ice calling her. She had always shown
a particular friendliness towards me so I hoped that this
might induce her to come in.

When I got nearer to her I could see she was now a very
frightened dog. For a while she kept about 200 yards away
from me, looking back over her shoulder, and each time I
attempted to close the distance she moved on. I abandoned
chasing to sit down. She stopped and sat down too. I talked
to her for some minutes then finally she got up and sneaked
back towards me.

At a few yards she stopped, looking at me distrustfully.
Her sides were heaving and she was shuddering with nervousness. It only needed the slightest shock to send her bounding
away in terror, and if that happened I would be obliged to
shoot. Very slowly, still talking softly, I took off my belt,
walking over to her. She sank down on her belly, her eyes
darting from side to side. At last I slipped the belt about her
neck and the crisis was over.

By the way she pulled at the belt on her way home, she
too seemed only too glad to be returning to the dog lines.
The opposition had been heavier than she had expected. But
once back, it was easily seen that she had not learnt her
lesson, and that if she got loose again there would be no
hesitation in her future actions. Mentally, we added another
star to Helen's rating and with it a rope collar to supplement
her leather one by way of insurance.

The new sea ice seemed to have come to stay. There was
an unbroken sheet to the horizon and near us it was twenty
inches thick. It was just possible that the route westward by
the sea ice had reformed. Accordingly Marret sent Lépineux
and I northward with a team to Pointe Eba to investigate
conditions there, before deciding whether to go by the plateau
or by the sea ice. We camped the first night at Ile Fram as

Rivolier and I had done a month previously. When we got there I searched for our old camp beside the island. It no longer existed. When the sea ice went the little bit of ice against the island which we had considered 'safe' had gone with it. This time we made sure of our camp, driving the dogs up on to the island itself. Here we found a colony of Weddel seals and their pups. They were newly born, in fact some were born during the few days we were in the vicinity. The mothers were great and ungainly creatures like all seals, but the new-born pups were the softest and prettiest little creatures in the world. Not much larger than a spaniel dog, they were protected by the softest grey-brown dappled fur and when we approached they showed no fear, gazing at us in wonder with great limpid brown eyes. We had planned to kill a seal for dog food but all we could find were mothers with pups. Hardened as both of us were to seal-killing we could not face killing a mother or one of these delightful little creatures.

The next day found us running north to Pointe Eba. There was no need to shout orders to Fram, he seemed to know where we were going and headed direct for the point. At exactly the spot where we had stopped on the last trip near the edge of open water, Fram decided his contract was completed and halted. He seemed most surprised when we wanted to go farther, and took it as a piece of underhand dealing. We continued a few miles more, to be sure that the ice was in all along the coast, then turned and raced back to Ile Fram. Here, we radioed back that it was possible, as far as we could see, to use the sea ice westward.

The following day it snowed heavily, and a yard-thick carpet of soft snow lay on the ice. We were then held up two more days by bad weather. It was a weary trip back. In the soft snow the dogs were down to their bellies, and we floundered alongside the sledge, sinking thigh deep in it. Only by resting the dogs every few hundred yards could we make progress. This fall of snow cancelled our favourable report on the sea ice, for a fall of soft snow insulates the ice from the cold air, and the warm sea beneath the ice begins to destroy it. Consequently the journey westward was definitely planned to take place on the plateau.

Almost immediately, Lépineux, Prévost and Duhamel left with Fram's team for Pointe Géologie, to begin marking a route for the weasels out through the crevassed zone which led up from the coast to the plateau proper. This was a most important reconnaissance, for on it largely depended the success of the journey to the west. Where the ice sheet inclines sharply from the plateau in the last twenty miles to the coast, it breaks over irregularities in the underlying land into great splits known as crevasses. These can vary from mere cracks to awesome chasms, a hundred feet wide, running for many miles, and a thousand feet deep. Usually crevasses are hidden from view by the bridge of snow that forms over them, and though some are obvious, a large number can only be located by proving with an ice-axe. For the weasels, crevassing represents a very real danger. The three-ton machines, passing over one of these wide bridges, would cause any insurance company to ask a high premium. It was the task of the weasel route party to locate and mark the most suitable and safest route available, until they cleared this dangerous coastal zone and emerged on the plateau proper, where the great depth of permanent snow minimized the danger of crevasses. Once this was done they were to establish a depot tent and return to base.

They were soon back for a second dog team, for the going in the soft snow was too heavy for their single team. Rivolier went with them driving Bjorn's team. Ifaut, the bitch of Bjorn's team, was sick and had to be replaced with Bobby from Pickles' team. We chose poor Bobby because he was so terrorized by Nick, and considered he would cause little trouble in a new team, being so downtrodden normally. He didn't. As Rivolier disappeared into the distance, we could see all his team bunched up together pulling, except for Bobby, who was at the end of his trace, behind the sledge, being towed along resisting strenuously. Everybody spoke highly of Fram. On the steep grades, ploughing through soft snow, he was magnificent. Whenever the sledge bogged down, he would back right against the sledge, then launch himself against the trace in a burst of energy to get the sledge under way once more. Prévost, who had always claimed Bjorn's team to be our best, had to admit that Fram's had now won top place.

Lépineux walked in on us one night, leading a limping Astro. Astro's paw was badly torn and crushed, and Lépineux, considering him too valuable a dog to risk, made a long walk back by night, leading him. Fram had done the damage. Being unused to using the team, they had tied up Fram the night before, a thing I never did. Astro, emboldened by the fact that Fram could not reach him, had commenced paying attentions to Helen. Fram screamed with impotent rage, leaping against his chain. Astro, further heartened by his continued safety, barked back defiance at Fram, while Fram worked himself to a pitch of raging fury, jumping against his chain to get at Astro.

Then Fram's chain broke!

It was a pity, because Astro was one of our best dogs, and needed for the main journey. He looked very forlorn, alone in the empty section of the dog lines that belonged to his team, licking his paw, and howling with misery at being out of the team. At intervals he would leap wildly against his chain, trying to break loose so that he could rejoin them. Nothing existed for Astro except the team; away from them he was lonely and miserable. To cheer him up we put the sick bitch, Ifaut, alongside him, so the two were able to commiserate with each other.

The weather was improving as the season advanced. It

had been noticeably warmer when I was away with Lépineux. The tent had been warm and dry, yet only a month previously with Rivolier, it had been cold and chill, with an inch of frost rime and ice coating the walls. And now, during the period that the weasel route party were away, we were blessed with a period of clear skies, light winds and general summery conditions at the base. This made us wonder when we received the nightly wireless signal from them, not much more than twenty miles away, continually reporting blizzard and bad weather conditions. However the night that they came in explained everything. At the base it had been calm and almost sultry, if a temperature of minus ten can be called that, and we had been wandering around in light jerseys. They came in from just twenty-five miles away and they were like beings out of another world. We had forgotten what it was like to see men with drift and ice driven into their clothes and beards, but they had it. And their dogs were so encrusted with ice as to remind us of our trip northward over the sea ice near mid-winter.

Life in the hut had been strange while they had been away. Each of us remaining, Marret, Vincent, and myself, had always been the ones away normally, and we were used to a hut full of people, the whole seven of us. With only three, it seemed deserted. Also we were, without fear of challenge, the three untidiest members of the party, and in our hands the accumulation of clothing and odds and ends in heaps in the hut began to get out of hand. We reduced our meals to one per day to ease the housework, but were still losing. The only advantage of the chaos was that for the first time in months we could find things in the hut. Before, when all was shipshape and tidy under more capable hands, we were forever losing things. Now we could lay our hands on anything we wanted without hesitation. Vincent would come in for his gloves, for example. No fruitless searching now. Straight for a pile of clothing in the corner of the hut, and after throwing aside half a dozen other items, he would emerge triumphant.

Just the same we were glad to see the others return. As the days passed, conditions inside the hut were getting further and further beyond us. We were seriously considering abandoning the hut and taking up fresh quarters in the weasel parked outside.

I, personally, was more glad than the other, I had missed the dogs.

The weasel route party had done a very good piece of work. They had marked out a route, with bamboo flags every half mile, from Pointe Géologie to a place they called Camp 6, thirty-two kilometres away. As far as they knew the route was clear of crevassing, except at one zone about ten kilometres out which all agreed was rather doubtful. Their side of it had been done. Now the way was open for our main western journey. This was planned to take place in a week's time. Its object was to strike south-west on the plateau and then to descend to the coast in a north-westerly direction, rejoining it at the border of French and Australian Antarctic Territory. Once there, the coast would be surveyed and mapped.

The personnel were to be Marret, Vincent, Rivolier and myself and for transport we would use two weasels supported by two teams of six dogs. Now the plan was decided, we busied ourselves with the final preparations.

The teams to go were to be Fram's and elements óf Bjorn's. This gave us one very strong team or alternatively two light teams of six and five dogs respectively. The plan was that the strong team of eight dogs headed by Fram would pull a loaded sledge behind the weasels, while the three remaining dogs would be attached to the weasel sledges running free of load to keep them always fresh. Fram's team was reconstituted as follows;

Fram   Leader
Astro   Lieutenant
Helen   Bitch
Seismo
Roald
Wild   suitable for working in the
        second team under Bjorn.
Pomme
Maru   same 'remark' as for Wild.

Bjorn and the two inseparables made the reserve. Maru and
Wild, both being easy-going dogs, could be switched across
to join these three to make the second team.

We took care in the selection of the teams for the western
journey. It was a long call back to the days when all the
dogs looked alike to us and we could not remember their
names. Now we knew each dog as a distinct personality, in
fact it is safe to say that we knew the character of each dog
much better than we knew the character of our fellow men.
Although we had twenty-two dogs, only half of these were
first-class animals. Some were axiomatic, the stalwarts like
Bjorn, Fram and Astro, but there were doubtful members
in the final group, particularly Pomme and Roald. Roald,
because he was young and by nature a craven, was thought
not tough enough to last out a serious journey. Pomme was a
replica of old Aspirin, and everyone knew Aspirin's record,
with only one journey to his credit, and from that he came
back a passenger on the sledge. Also Pomme's heavy body
and long hair were great handicaps on the plateau. His great
weight made him clumsy, and where the lighter dogs
jumped obstacles Pomme floundered over them painfully,
while the fine drift snow drove into his long, wooly hair to
form into ice, so that by the end of day he would be carrying
a coat of mail of ice weighing up to forty pounds.

The remaining dogs under Pickles were to be left at camp

to act as our reserve transport in case of emergency. Georges Lépineux volunteered to look after this group in our absence and immediately began to speak of 'my team.'

'My team' at this stage were the dregs of the dog lines. All of Pickles' team were now old, and through lack of use their training had gone to pieces. Besides Pickles' team, the dogs left behind were either sick or useless, or expecting pups. But to Georges, they were a fine body of dogs. The poorest specimen was Nelson, the halfwit. Nelson had always been a peculiar dog both in manner and appearance. Lately he had been getting worse. His health was deteriorating rapidly, and his mental powers were waning in proportion.

Georges waxed enthusiastic over 'my team,' and claimed that Nelson was a beautiful and intelligent dog with his obvious virtues undeveloped through lack of understanding.

'*Quel beau chien!*' Georges was wont to remark as we looked at Nelson.

Lately Nelson had been breaking loose at regular intervals. I suggested to Georges, since Nelson was his dog, that the danger to the penguins was now Georges's responsibility. Georges was most indignant that anyone would so much as suspect a paragon like Nelson of being a danger to the Emperors. It seemed not, for as soon as he was loose Nelson would wander up the dog lines and sit down near Judy, remaining there for hours on end watching her, with the same odd light in his eyes as he had as he edged in behind a man with his fangs showing. That seemed harmless enough.

There was another group we knew as Paton's team. These were Paton, Janet and Bora the three pups, and chained with them the old retired warrior, Boss. The pups were still too young for work, and Boss, of course, was now too old. Paton and Bora were firm friends while Boss and Janet seemed to get on well enough too. However in young Paton were stirring the instincts of the pack. He seemed already to be visualizing himself as the leader of a team and he objected to Boss. Consequently from time to time he used to break loose and attack Boss, as the only dog in his team. Paton usually won, since Boss was now a pale shadow of his former self. He had lost all his interest in the other dogs and now was only fit to laze in the weak spring sunshine and the highlight of each day came when a passing man stopped to pat him.

A little earlier, with the coming of spring, the old blood had run a little quicker than of late, and Boss's eyes grew brighter and there was a travesty of spring in his movements. He was loose for a few minutes and decided to visit his old team (now Fram's). He sallied across to the dog lines, tail held high and with a jaunty step. It seemed he felt so well as to try to recapture his lost ascendancy. It was a sad affair. Back with the pups, he sat licking his many wounds sadly. He never went near the grown dogs again, and even to the quarter-grown Paton, he was poor sport. The old warrior had come to the evening of his days. It was certain that at the end of the year we would have to shoot him, and for that reason we did our best to give him his last months of comfort. Whenever posible we took him for walks and for the rest of the time he lay on the rocks enjoying a well-earned rest.

Aspirin, too, was receiving special treatment. In front of the hut was an old landing barge, left there purposely to act as a super rubbish bin. In this was the accumulated kitchen and other refuse of many long months. To this barge we chained Aspirin and there he was able to lie in a delectable mass of selected filth such that he had never dreamed of in his wildest longings. Each day we would see him selecting particularly loathsome pieces of refuse and lining them in front of him in case of need during the day, before flopping in beatific slumber in the cesspit he had constructed for himself in the barge. It was paradise on earth for Aspirin.

At this time, however, the future for all the dogs seemed

dark. The base was to be closed down at the end of the year and there was to be no relief party to take over from us. As yet no satisfactory arrangements could be made for the dogs and the shadow of death hung over all of them. We could see looming up ahead of us in a few months the ghastly job of shooting all our four-footed comrades. The best we could hope for was to save the young and vigorous dogs. The old stalwarts who had given their best for the lest three years for their masters, Boss, Pickles, Judy, Nick, Bobby, Nelson and (although hardly a stalwart) Aspirin—all would have to be dispatched.

It is easy to see from where the term 'a dog's life' came. The coiner of the phrase must have been thinking of sledge dogs. They are born in conditions of cold and misery, and struggle in their first months for bare existence with very mixed success.

As soon as they are strong enough they are put in training to take their place in the team. From then on they live on a chain, in the open, racked by wind and snow and bitter cold, their only shelter the snow that buries them as the blizzard rages. They suffer the stern discipline of the driver and the sterner discipline of their leader. They are fed on frozen seal meat, frozen so hard that chips fly from the axe that cuts its. Their only way of eating this is to thaw it with their tongues and bodies little by little. They slake their thirst with dry cold snow. Their only relief from boredom is battle with other dogs with, as prize, the dubious reward of leadership of the team. This, once he has gained it, a dog holds easily at first. Then, as the years slip by, the battles become harder, till at last some strong young dog beats him and the team fall upon him as one, and he is a shattered wreck of a dog like Boss.

Is it any wonder that the husky looks forward to pulling a sledge in the same way as a normal dog loves a walk with its master?

Not that sledging can be described as an enjoyable existence. Every day that the weather permits travel, the team
pulls a heavily laden sledge at walking pace from twenty to
thirty miles. There is day after day of it, and any dog that
becomes sick or is injured cannot be rested. He must pull as
long as he is physically able and when he can no longer do
so, he must be killed and his body fed to the others. Twenty
to thirty miles every day and then at the close of it, each
dog is fed a pound of concentrated food and sleeps staked
out in the open on the snow, with no protection from the icy
winds. In the morning he goes back into harness, now frozen
hard as a board, and the next day's march begins. There are
no rewards for the husky; he has the job to do and is expected to do it. When he is no longer capable there is no
leisured old age, only execution.

So it is not extraordinary that, with such a life, the softer
side of the dog's character vanishes, to be replaced by cruel
and brutal ways more suited to the existence that he leads.
Since in this breed there was the wolf not very far back on
the family tree, the characteristics of the wolf overide those
of the dog. He no longer barks, if ever he did. His cry is the
mournful howling of the wolf. The team and the pack become identified as one, for each dog lives, not as an individual, but as a member of the team. Alone he is lost and
troubled, he needs to run in his place with his team. All the
dogs fight grim battles in order to unseat their leader and
establish themselves in his place. This can be very annoying
for their trainer. He may have an excellent dog, highly intelligent and well trained, ideally suited to be a leader; but if
that dog is unable to assert his superiority in battle, the
team will refuse him in favour of a great idiot of a dog whose
only claim to the position is his strength and skill in fighting.

The innate brutality of the husky continually shocks a
man. They seem to have an irresistible urge to savage anything weak and helpless. There is a dog that seems to be

gentle, it seems to be quiet enough to be the companion of a young child. The man would be prepared to swear by its gentleness, until the day a small pup walked past it, and the mask of the dog slipped as the jaws of the wolf closed like a steel trap on the little body. I was forever getting shocks of this sort. Boss was a typical case. Old Boss had never been known to kill anything. Like Fram and Ifaut, he seemed cast in a gentler mould. On walks with me, I used to watch him pass an occupied nest of a giant petrel, with barely a glance at the fluffy chick, a tempting morsel that no other of the dogs could miss. But one day, Boss ran into a group of soft, fluffy Emperor penguin chicks, and then his record, too, was blotted with murder.

We often speculated as to whether they would turn on a badly injured driver if he was on his own; a question, fortunately, that we never resolved. I do not think so, since from puppyhood they have been taught that the one unforgiveable sin is to bite a man. After a year with this group I was bitten once, and that by my old friend Fram. It was a mistake on his part. I was leading another dog when Fram leapt at him, but misjudged his stroke. Immediately, he cowered back, struck by the enormity of his crime and fearful of the retribution that inevitably must come. But any one of us could wade into a snarling, seething mass of ten dogs, all engaged in a desperate free-for-all, and cuff the blood-mad brutes with his bare hands and run not the least risk of being bitten. I would much rather break up a brawl between half a dozen huskies than try to settle a difference of opinion between two Pekinese.

The dog sledges were repaired and packed with stores in preparation for the western journey, while Vincent and Marret worked on the two weasels. Each machine was checked over thoroughly, for the polar plateau is an uncomfortable place in which to make mechanical repairs. Inside the hut, another group were busy weighing and packing rations. These were packed in cloth bags, each containing the complete ration for three men for one day. The basic food of the ration was pemmican, a concentrated mixture of powdered lean meat and fat, which analyzes as forty-two per cent fat and forty-seven per cent protein. This was supplemented by butter, biscuits in quantity, oatmeal, milk powder, sugar, chocolate, coffee and cocoa. There was a great deal to be done before we could start up the weasels, cry 'Mush' to the dogs, and be on our way.

We had very limited stocks of dog pemmican and this food had to be reserved for the time when the dogs would be operating on their own, away from the weasels. While they were still with the weasels we planned to feed them on seal meat carried for them on the vehicles. This meant a special seal hunt to supply the meat for this need. Five Weddel seals were shot and their carcasses dragged back to camp. Then all the flesh was filleted of bones, to avoid carrying unnecessary weight, and the fillets cut into rations. These hunks of meat were left out overnight to freeze into blocks, then packed in cardboard cylinders of a hundred and forty pounds weight for transport.

Apart from the work of actual preparation, there was still the routine work to be done. For the group going west, there was another odd task. Since they expected to be away about two months, it was well possible that by the time they saw the camp again, the relief ship would have arrived, so each of us going had to complete his station work and pack his personal gear before he left.

Finally all was done that should be done. The two weasels were in near perfect order. The weasel sledges and barges were loaded with food, fuel, and general gear, and the spare dog sledge was carried on top of one of the sledge loads, while the first dog sledge stood by fully loaded, only needing the dogs to be harnessed for us to move off.

Marret had set November 5th as the day of departure, but it was late in the afternoon of that day before the last arrangements were completed and all was ready for departure. Marret always believed that the most difficult thing to do was to start, so even though only a few hours of light remained, the party climbed into the weasels and the procession moved off.

Hirondelle, our original weasel, led the group, towing a heavily laden barge, ironing out a track for Coccinelle, to follow. Coccinelle was even more heavily laden, towing a barge-load of stores and a sledge carrying a ton of gasoline. Attached to the fuel sledge were the three reserve dogs, Bjorn, Milk and Tiki. Finally, bringing up the rear, was Fram's team of eight dogs, driven by me, and dragging their own loaded sledge.

Down the slope from the hut, the convoy moved, down over the tide crack on to the sea ice, thence across the bay towards the setting sun. Behind us, Lépineux, Prévost and Duhamel waved their best wishes, and ahead were the unknown lands to the west of Pointe Géologie. The roaring of the weasel motors broke the cold silence of the Antarctic evening, and now and then, as the dogs settled down to pulling, one of them whimpered. The sledge runners made a soft swishing as they slid over the cold dry snow, and walking alongside the sledge, I slipped on my gloves and pulled up the hood of my parka, for the wind blowing off the plateau was cold, chilling bare flesh to the bone.

The journey had really begun.

8

Westward on the Plateau

We made camp that night at Pointe Géologie. A very
different Pointe Géologie to what it had been when we
camped there with the dogs before the mid-winter journey
to Port Martin. Not only was it pleasant to stroll around outside after the evening meal, but where it had been dead and
lifeless now the Adelie penguins were everywhere, trotting
officiously up from the sea ice to where the females were
sitting each on a little nest of pebbles, quarrelling, fishwife
fashion, with her neighbours.

The dogs were chained along the edge of the rocks just
underneath the penguins, and several of the little black and
white people paid a high price for their inquisitiveness or
quarrelsomeness. I watched one such tragedy occur. Just
above Milk and Tiki were two pairs of Adelies who resented
the presence of the two dogs. After a lot of chattering one
penguin advanced on the dogs, flippers outstretched and
neck fluffed up with anger. Behind him the remaining three
hurled abuse at the dogs and encouragement to their champion. As soon as he was in reach the two dogs sprang. In
their over-eagerness, the dogs hindered each other so that in
the confusion the penguin was thrown clear, badly wounded
but still alive. He stood swaying weakly from side to side
undecided, then pushing his flippers out and fluffing up his
bleeding neck he returned to the attack. This time Milk and

Tiki did not miss. A bloodstain on the ice and a few feathers were all that remained of the courageous little creature.

The remaining three penguins went into conference. It appeared that the two females were in favour of continuing the attack but the surviving male, on whom the active side of the operation fell, did not seem to share their enthusiasm. At last, the two females had their way, and they pushed the unwilling warrior forward. The two dogs sank on their bellies and waited. There was a brief melee out of which a wounded and bleeding penguin somehow emerged alive. He fled, squawking with terror, into the middle of the rookery. Here the last act of the tragedy was played out. The other penguins fell on him and the defeated gladiator was pecked to death by his fellows. There was nothing we could have done to avert the death of the two penguins. If we had saved them then they would have certainly returned to the attack while we slept.

The next morning we got under way at an early hour. At the beginning of the journey was a steep slope leading up a thousand feet to the top of the plateau. The weasels could not pull their heavy loads up this slope, so we relayed the loads from Géologie up to the beginning of the doubtful zone reported by the reconnaisance party. At this point the men saw signs of crevassing, but there was considerable snow lying which hid the crevasses themselves. At the end of the day I was following the last loaded weasel with the dog teams and had fallen behind. When I arrived at the crevassed zone I saw Coccinelle on its side at a dangerous angle. Vincent, who was driving it, had run for some distance alongside a hidden crevasse, and finally the track of the weasel had broken through the masking snow bridge. Now the weasel was perched precariously on the edge. The crevasse was a big one, about thirty feet wide and a thousand feet deep. The weasel, in slipping sideways, had wedged

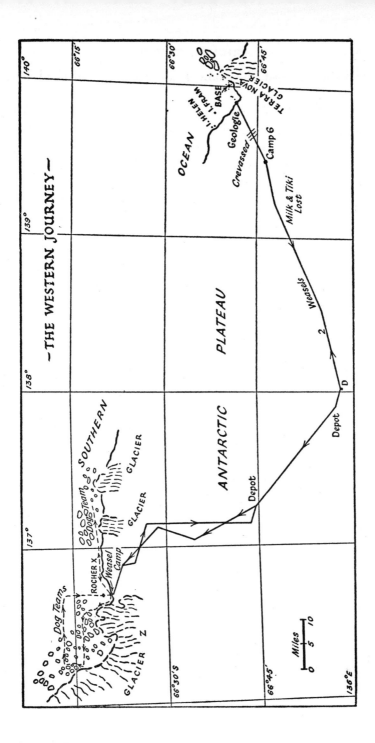

~THE WESTERN JOURNEY~

its cabin against the snow bridge and its fall had been arrested.

With the aid of jacks and pieces of timber Marret, working on the snow bridge and using an alpine rope as security in case the whole bridge collapsed, succeeded in jacking the weasel up until it was once more upright. Then, by attaching the surviving weasel, it was dragged clear of the danger.

An investigation of our surroundings found another great crevasse ten yards on the other side of us and our camp was revealed to be only a few yards of sound ice between crevasses of great dimensions. We were not very happy about the situation. The only way to go forward was to drive the two and a half ton weasels over several of these large crevasses. Some of the snow bridges over these crevasses were so weak that a man on foot would break through, while in others the whole crevasse was so well bridged that the gap was virtually chocked with snow and a locomotive could be driven across. In an old crevasse there is such a mass of snow held up that the mere two and a half tons of the weasel is insignificant. At least that is the theory of scrambling a weasel across a snow bridge. Unfortunately, it is impossible to tell by inspection whether the bridge is old enough to bear the weight of the weasel. The only way to be definitely sure is to drive the machine across. There can be no doubt once this has been done.

We went to sleep that night with several such crossings ahead of us on the morrow.

It was half-loads forward again the next day, a slow and worrying business. A man walked ahead on foot, attached to the leading weasel by an alpine rope, carefully probing the route ahead to locate the crevasses. Then the strongest part of each bridge was found and the weasel signalled forward. The driver then hoped for the best as the weasel crawled slowly over the abyss. It was nerve-wracking enough to watch, but the driver was labouring under the heaviest

strain. Marret described the sensation as similar to flying a
bomber in heavy flak. Either you were hit or you were not.
There was not a great deal that could be done about it. Not
even evasive action. Just sit tight and hope for the best.

This is what the onlooker sees. On each side of the crevasse
are bamboos marking its edges, making it easy to see the
whole extent of the crevasse. At each edge there is a weak
section where the snow in the bridge has contracted and
pulled away. The whole thing looks as though it only needs
a touch to send it avalanching into the depths below. The
driver engages his gears and approaches at a right angle
to the crevasse. The watchers hold their breath as the weasel
dips down off the firm ice on to the bridge. One track breaks
through the weak section of the edge, revealing a glimpse
of dark blue nothingness below it. The engine revs and the
tracks bite and the weasel crawls slowly over the bridge. It
reaches the other side and the bow of the machine goes up
as the tracks scramble on the far side. At last the weasel is
on firm ice once more and another crevasse is passed. The
man ahead goes on probing methodically with an ice-axe
for the next. It is very understandable that all breathed a
sigh of relief when this zone of crevasses was at last left
behind.

We had intended, once safe ground was gained, to deposit
the half-loads and return to the beginning of this zone to
pick up the other half of the loads that night, but the weather
closed down rapidly so we were obliged to camp enroute.
The only thing that worried us was that the dogs had been
left at the remaining half-loads and needed to be fed. However, they were very self-sufficient animals after three years
in this part of the world, and we were sure that they would
be able to look after themselves for a day or two. Late the
following day we reached the dogs again. They were none
the worse for being left alone, but for all that glad enough
to see us. The recrossing of the crevassed zone held no worries

now. Having successfully passed it once, another crossing did not offer any problems.

There is an awful sameness about the polar plateau. There are no valleys or hills, few outcrops, nothing but a waste of snow and ice stretching to the horizon, undulating so gently as to be barely perceptible. A photograph taken at any point on a two-hundred-mile journey would be duplication of the view at all other points along the route. Bereft of all landmarks, it seems more desolate than any desert. At least in a desert there are changes of soil, sand and colour, while here there is nothing but wind-furrowed ice and snow stretching to infinity.

There can be nothing more boring than a well-planned journey on the plateau. One is inclined to welcome little mishaps as a break in the tedium of travel. The surface is difficult for machines; the ever-present wind cuts the snow into sastrugi as much as a yard high and these furrows are packed by the wind until the snow is as hard as marble. The weasels jolt and stagger their way forward. Nothing can be held in place inside the cabins in the continual jolting. I made a seventeen-mile journey during the war in a jeep over a corduroy road in the jungle and thought the experience the nadir of discomfort when travelling. But a weasel journey on medium sastrugi makes the jeep trip a journey to be remembered with comparative pleasure.

My three companions took the brunt of this. I made most of the journey driving my dog team in the wake of the weasels. This was a sinecure, since in that vast expanse of nothingness there was nothing to attract the dogs' attention but the weasels ahead of them. There was no driving to do; just a matter of walking alongside the sledge from dawn to dusk. Sometimes, especially early in the day when the dogs were fresh, we would be close behind the weasels; in fact, it was necessary to halt the dogs from time to time or we would overtake them. But, in the evenings, as fatigue claimed the dogs and the weasels which knew no fatigue would be many miles ahead of us, we would find ourselves, the dog team and I, quite alone on the plateau, following the tracks of the weasels.

It was a rather pleasant sensation to halt the team for a rest, scan the empty horizon, and feel completely alone in the icy wastes. There was a cold beauty about its very desolateness, not a beauty of form but one of texture; the sky could be so intensely blue, the snow so intensely white and the sastrugi lay in chaotic patterns to the limit of sight. Cutting across the irregularity was the one mark of man, the even, regular tracks of the weasels stretching ahead towards the unknown. Then, suddenly realizing that the weasels were steadily drawing away from us, I would break our meditation with a crack of a whip and we would be off again chasing those tracks until we finally caught up with the machines at their camp for the night.

The miles between us and the base camp increased. Some days the weather kept us holed up in the weasels while the blizzard raged, other days the visibility was so bad that travel was risky. These were flat white days with a shadowless uniform layer of cloud stretching over the sky and blending into the featureless surface.

The weasels shed tracks frequently in the high sastrugi, necessitating delays while the tracks were refitted. Sometimes a weasel, clambering over high-angled sastrugi, slipped and fell over on its side and the machine had to be jacked back on its tracks and the sastrugi broken down with picks and shovels. Before a quarter of the journey was done we had smashed one main spring and our only spare had been used to replace it. The other mishaps had no permanent effects but the smashing of suspension springs could mean abandoning one of the weasels on the plateau.

Accidents happened to the dogs as well. Milk and Tiki

were running tied to the rear sledge of the rear weasel. My team following could see the tails of these two wagging ahead of them and were continually trying to overtake the weasels in order to attack them. Both Milk and Tiki were aware of the danger that threatened them in the slavering jaws of the team behind and whimpered in fear whenever the following team closed up on them. It took all my strength on the sledge brake to hold them as they got close to the weasels. One day I was too slow with the brake. Tiki saved himself by leaping on to the weasel barge but poor Milk was too slow. Eight pairs of steely jaws closed on him and he screamed in agony. The sledge came to a halt but Vincent, driving the weasel, was unable to hear my shouting or the clamour behind him and continued on. My dog sledge, was loaded with 700 pounds of freight and the weasel was towing it, but the connecting link between the two was poor Milk's body held by the jaws of the eight dogs. At last I managed to attract Vincent's attention and we pulled Milk clear. He was horribly mangled with deep wounds several inches long where the dogs' teeth had dragged through skin and flesh. Ordinarily the only thing to do would be to shoot the animal and put him out of his misery. If he had been on a purely dog journey this would have been done without hesitation but with the weasels we could carry a sick dog, so Rivolier attempted to sew up his gaping wounds.

For days he lay on the weasel sledge, a miserable heap of canine suffering, being painfully jolted as the sledge moved forward and squealing with terror as he heard the baying of the team behind him. A man with such wounds would have been in hospital for months, if not dead. But a fortnight later Milk's wounds were sufficiently healed for him to take his place in harness and pull his weight in the team.

Tiki was fully aware of the danger from the following team. He had evolved a quick manœuvre under the weasel sledge that put him in a position where he could only be attacked with difficulty. Bjorn, on the other hand, who was also attached to a weasel sledge at this time, always stood his ground and met the attackers face to face. He was still king dog and none of the dogs, including Fram, were confident enough to tackle the doughty warrior. But I could see Bjorn was worried. He was still confident he could handle any one of those dogs alone, but he was also very much aware that if the whole team fell on him at once he would share Milk's fate and worse.

Fram was trying to bring just this state of affairs to pass. He was forever disregarding orders to halt and trying to overrun the weasel sledges and engage Bjorn, supported by the whole team. But each time, when within a straw's width of success, his courage would fail him and he was afraid to signal the general attack by joining battle with Bjorn.

Bjorn's lack of intelligence was clearly demonstrated on this journey. He was attached by collar and chain to a weasel sledge carrying a ton of gasoline. He could run alongside this sledge, or, if he wished, jump aboard and be carried with it. Poor Bjorn had been brought up as a well-trained husky. The first lesson he had ever been taught was that a husky's job when attached to a sledge is to pull. He had never forgotten this. Somewhere in the fuzzy recesses of his brain he had come to associate the whirr of the weasel self-starter with the command to mush. So each time he heard the starter turn he would jump down from the sledge, put his back into it and pull.

In these hundred weary miles of back-breaking work poor Bjorn never realized that it was the weasel and not he that dragged that massive load! And this despite the fact that alongside him were Milk and Tiki, riding effortlessly on top of the weasel sledges.

Pomme was making heavy weather of it. As anticipated, the plateau drift played havoc with his long curly fur. On the plateau in Adélie Land, even on fine days, there is a continual ground drift of windblown snow sweeping waist-high over the surface. This wind did not worry the Greenland dogs with their short hair. They all iced up to a certain extent, but with poor Pomme the drift drove deep into his thick fur and in a very short time he was clad in a sheet of heavy ice. His harness was always frozen stiff because the warmth of his body would not reach it through his coat of ice. Every movement must have been agonizing, with the stiff harness cutting into his flesh and the ice pulling at his fur. At times it was impossible to get him in and out of harness. This was by no means his only trouble. He became so changed in appearance that the other dogs grouped against him. His only friend was the driver, and whenever the sledge halted Pomme would edge back to be under the shelter of the driver's whip. Fram seemed to have a deep-rooted animosity for the big dog and bullied him whenever he got the opportunity. The team seemed to decide with common accord, whenver they were standing, that they would attack Pomme. The coat of ice that brought on this animosity was of great help to him then. Dropped on his belly with his head tucked between his front paws, Pomme was a tortoise and the attackers usually failed to hurt him.

But Pomme confounded our predictions that he would not last more than a fortnight. He had a great heart, and no matter how difficult the going he somehow managed to shamble his way courageously on. He was fast becoming the hero of the journey.

One dog was failing and it came as a surprise to us. Wild, the big gangling dog of Fram's team, was going downhill rapidly. On short trips he had always seemed a first-class dog but apparently he did not possess the stamina for a serious journey. His ribs began to show through his shaggy fur and his trace was more often slack than taut. There was no life in his movements, just weary resignation to the work.

On the contrary Roald, my erstwhile pet and the youngest dog of the group, improved as the days went by. Before, he had been the butt of continual attacks by the others, but now that Pomme was receiving all the attention Roald began to settle down to his place in the team and to enjoy the vigorous work.

Fram was magnificent. The hard core of the team was Fram, Astro, Seismo and Helen. The other dogs only made up the number. Helen's capacity for work was insatiable. She may have been a continual source of trouble about the camp, but in the field there was no other dog that could pull as she did for so long and so hard. She was always dead ahead of the sledge, belly low, legs outspread and her trace at taut as a violin string. When the team stopped for a rest, most would flop on the snow panting, or at best stand in their traces gulping lungfuls of frozen air, but little black Helen would be leaping against the trace, yelping in anxiety to be under way again.

By previous custom Fram was never chained during the halts. Any other dog but Fram would have abused such a privilege by breaking into sledge loads to seal food, but Fram was intelligent enough to realize that if he was once caught raiding the sledges his freedom would vanish. In retrospect I find it strange that while every other dog on that journey lost weight in the seven weeks we were away, Fram on the contrary waxed plumper. However, Fram, as I say, was never seen raiding the sledges.

Bjorn, on the other hand, fell in for severe punishment on more than one occasion. On several occasions as we broke camp we found Bjorn nosing in the tattered fragments of one of our three-day ration bags. This puzzled us, since chained as he was it was well nigh impossible for the big dog to reach the rations. We had a sneaking suspicion that Fram was at the bottom of the mystery. It was just possible that Fram had raided the stores, stolen a bag of rations and, having selected all the tasty items, had presented Bjorn with the bag containing the less attractive parts. Bjorn, being of low intelligence, had never learnt to fear the Greeks even when bearing gifts, and as a result while Fram sat by, the picture of saintly innocence, Bjorn received Fram's punishment at the price of a few dried fruits and a packet of cocoa.

I always felt sorry for the dogs. On a journey they were always fed the bare minimum, living on the verge of starvation in a state of perpetual hunger. The reason for this apparently needless maltreatment of the animals is a matter of sledging economies. Granting each dog 1 lb. of concentrated food per day, as was our dog ration, with a team of eight dogs on a six weeks' journey, 336 pounds of dog food have to be loaded on the sledge before anything else. Add to this 170 pounds of man food and 40 pounds of fuel for the primuses and the sledge load begins to take form. Each dog can pull 70 pounds on the sledge, giving a total load of 560 lbs.

Adding up these totals

Dog food	336 lb.
Man food	170 lb.
Fuel	40 lb.
Tent	30 lb.
	516 lb.

leaves a narrow margin of 44 lb. for instruments and all other necessary gear. Thus the dogs must be fed a bare minimum of food when travelling.

On this particular journey, since the weasels were carrying the dogs' food, their ration was four pounds of seal meat per day. Even with this the animals were very hungry. At each camp on the plateau the sequence of events was similar. The weasels would have been halted pointed down-wind at the point selected for the night's camp when the dog team caught up with them. The dogs soon learnt that to find the two weasels drawn up in this formation signified the end of the day's labour and a meal. So despite the fact that they had been staggering with weariness an hour before, the moment they saw the halted weasels they would flog their weary bodies into a shambling trot to close the distance between them and rest and food as quickly as possible.

One of the problems of plateau travel was the drift that swept continually across the surface, burying in a few days any obstacle that stood above the uniform surface. When the weasels halted, this driving snow eddying about them built up huge dunes of snow down-wind of the machines in a matter of hours. I have seen such dunes six feet high, twenty feet across at the base and stretching for miles, all thrown up during a night's halt. Thus, anything left in the lee of an obstruction was immediately buried.

For this reason the dogs were always driven a hundred yards to windward of the weasel camp, where the sledge was halted facing down the wind to present the minimum obstacle to the drifting snow, and then they were staked down clear of the sledge. The next move was their feeding. For this purpose Fram would leave the team to accompany me to the weasel sledge carrying the dog food. The seal meat was cut in ration-size blocks and packed in waxed cardboard cylinders in which the meat had frozen into a rocklike conglomerate. Only hard blows with an axe could break each block free of the general mass, the container being hacked to pieces in the process. Each time the axe descended the howling of the half-starved dogs rose in volume as they leapt against their moorings in a frenzy of anticipation. Fram meticulously fielded each chip of frozen meat that flew from the axe; he had come to regard these as his perquisites. Then, as I spread the blocks of meat out on the snow to check that there was one for each dog, he carefully selected his own piece and trotted over to his place in the team alongside Helen. After I had distributed the food, all that remained to be done was to supervise the dogs to see that no dog went without because another stole his ration and to untangle the harness traces that had become twisted and knotted during the day's travel. Once this was done, I could clamber into No. 1 weasel where Marret would have already commenced heating our evening meal. The dogs would soon be curled up, back into the wind, asleep. The day was over for both men and dogs.

Of course at times things did not run quite so smoothly. When the main spring on one of the weasels was broken Marret and Vincent stayed working deep into the cold night to strip off the broken spring and replace it with the one spare we carried. Long after the last dog had settled down for the night, Marret and Vincent laboured on in the dark and cold with the drift snow swirling about them, while Rivolier and I stamped about to keep warm, offering our assistance. Marret remarked that it seemed colder for those doing nothing, but I couldn't agree with him, for handling steel tools and metal parts in a cramped position looked about as uncomfortable a task as one could imagine.

There were times too when the dogs caused trouble. One night the dogs were tied out and I was cutting up their meat as usual. Suddenly the pickets holding the leaping dogs' mooring line were dragged out by their concerted effort and the next moment an excited mass of dogs bore down on the sledges.

They swarmed over the weasel sledge in a wave, uncontrollable in their rush to find food. It was almost impossible to beat them off with a bamboo pole I grabbed from the sledge. While I was beating half of them away from the seal meat, the remaining half would be rummaging in our ration sacks. I was kept very busy for a few minutes, but not so busy as not to notice the wily Fram, profiting from the general confusion, also raiding the stores. One of the

men came to my aid and at last with our combined efforts
we managed to drive off the attackers. This done, it now was
necessary to mete out punishment. The dogs were all still
attached to their mooring line, which they had carried with
them. As I began punishing them, one by one, I saw Fram
from the corner of my eye, slinking away to about a hundred
yards distance. But, unfortunately for Fram, I had noticed
his surreptitious raiding, so on him as well as the others
fell the bamboo wand.

This travel on the plateau seemed endless. Only astronomical observations could tell us what movement we had
made each day. As a result of these we knew our own position exactly but, since we were covering new ground, this
did not help a great deal for we did not know the position
of our destination on the map.

We had one bad day near the end. The sastrugi had been
high and hard the previous day, though by careful driving
it had been possible to make progress. Overnight there was a
fall of fine, powdery snow, which filled the valleys in the
sastrugi, levelling them off. This seemed to promise an excellent travelling surface but, after the weasels had side-slipped
three times onto their sides, we decided to halt and pray for
wind to blow away this fine snow and expose the bare
sastrugi again. We realized that when the sastrugi had been
visible the weasel drivers were able to angle their approach
to meet each ridge at the best angle; now, travelling blind,
they would cut the sastrugi at all sorts of angles. Then, when
the weasels ran with one track supported on a ridge and the
other on the soft snow filling the trench between ridges, the
track supported on soft snow would drop, toppling the machine on its side. A two and a half ton machine toppled over
on its side presents a major piece of work for four men.
Only by dint of much shoveling and the slow judicious use
of jacks can the heavy machine be righted. One or two

such mishaps per day can be accepted as part of the normal problems of travel but this was too much.

Several days later the weasels were heading northward searching for the coast. The descent from three thousand feet of altitude to sea level was imperceptible. Only the steadily rising barometer, indicating loss of height, was a sure indication that we were nearing the sea. Otherwise the unchanging horizon of the plateau ice-cap was always with us. Travel was swifter, since before turning northwards a depot of fuel and food had been made and the weasels, lightened of their loads, were able to make quicker progress. The dogs were finding it increasingly difficult to keep up with the machines.

The first sure signs of the sea were a series of regular block-like shapes showing on the northern horizon. These were icebergs some forty miles from land. This first proof of our nearness to the coast was heartening to all. The conversation swung round to Adelie penguin eggs, fresh penguin steaks and seal meat. We felt certain that we would find Adelie penguins for they existed everywhere else along the coast. We hoped that perhaps we would find a second Emperor penguin rookery. After all why not here, if they were established at Pointe Géologie? In any case we were descending from the barren nothingness of the plateau to the sea and plenty. I promised each of my dogs his fill of seal meat the moment we found the coast and seals.

Gradually the panorama of the frozen sea opened up to us as we descended. First a few scattered icebergs on the horizon, then two great glacier tongues and finally the bay formed by the tongues of the glacier. On the left was the enormous glacier known as Glacier Z from aerial photographs of the Byrd Expedition (Operation High Jump). This was unbelievably large. Its face ran from the near distance and was still continuing at the far horizon. The vast field of bergs shed by it covered the face of the frozen sea. Somewhere still out of sight, tucked away in the bay between Glacier Z and the small glacier to the east, was a little island known as Rocher X from the same photographs. Opposite this was a little rocky cape on the coast we were to know as Nunatak Z.

We continued the descent as rapidly as possible, since all were anxious to reach the coast. The most hazardous part of the descent was a section where it became necessary to run parallel with the coast to make westing before the final descent. Here the machines were moving parallel to the coastal crevassing but fortunately this danger was passed without event. However, at midnight, when only ten miles from the coast Marret wisely halted his group. Although there was now no night, just an hour of so of twilight, visibility was poor, and that last ten-mile stretch, where the ice sheet sloped steeply to the coast, was almost certain to be dangerously crevassed. It was no place for tired but excited men in bad light.

The dogs were very tired. Even Fram did not muster the energy to join me when I went for their food. They all lay curled up with their backs to the driving snow to lie mutely waiting their meagre ration of rocklike seal meat.

The next day we were away early. Marret gave me permission to race ahead with the dogs, so that I could be at the nunatak at noon in order to make an observation for latitude when the sun was on the meridian. The weasels followed down the tracks of the dog sledge with Rivolier on foot ahead of them, secured by an Alpine rope to the leading weasel probing for hidden crevasses. In the descent with the dogs I marked each visible one with a flag as I passed it.

First, Rocher X peeped over the ice crest ahead. It was reassuring to see its dark, rocky form after these weeks of unbroken whiteness; a little later to the west I saw Nunatak Z. The dogs realized for the first time that we were at last off the plateau and broke into a flat run. As I had no wish to go hurtling off the edge of the coastal ice cliff, I let half the dogs out of the traces so that I would be able to control the sledge on the steep descent. So deeply was team life engrained in the liberated dogs that, after one brief scamper ahead, they halted and looked back at the sledge well behind them. Then, one by one, they regained the sledge, each taking his normal position with the team just as perfectly as if they had been still attached to it in harness.

Nunatak Z was a disappointment. Incredibly, there were no Adelie penguins. The only sign of life was two skua gulls cawing on top of the rocks. The frozen bay was bare of seals. There seemed to be something sinister about the place. At any other similar point on the coast the silence would be shattered by quarrelling penguins, sea birds would be sweeping through the air and seals would be dotted over the sea ice at this time of the year. Here there was nothing but these two nomadic gulls, whose home might be hundreds of miles away, for they are true nomads; Captain Scott saw one of these only a degree of latitude away from the Pole itself.

As soon as I had completed my observations I unloaded most of my sledge to run back to rejoin the weasels. On the descent I struck too far east of the direct route, so I made a short cut on a straight line to meet the weasels. However, I cut the weasel tracks behind them; they were progressing more rapidly than I had estimated, still following the sledge tracks.

Before I rejoined them Seismo had a shock that he probably still remembers. We were running across a zone of blue ice when we encountered a strip of snow about five feet wide, stretching across the ice sheet and slightly below the general surface level. Seismo should have known that this was a thin snow bridge over a crevasse. As it was, all the other dogs leaped the danger, landing on the firm ice on the other side. Seismo jumped only half way and the snow dissolved under his feet. In a cloud of snow he went hurtling into the dark abyss. Standing on the sledge I shot safely across, catching a momentary glimpse of Seismo dangling ten feet down in his harness with dark blue nothingness beneath him, much too startled even to yelp. The next second he came shooting out of the crevasse like a jack-in-the-box as the onward movement of the sledge and dogs dragged him back to safety by his trace. Before he could collect his wits he was back in his place in the team pulling and wearing a most puzzled expression, no doubt wondering whether he had imagined the whole episode.

We found the weasels pulled up at the nunatak. Rivolier was already sitting on the snow plucking two dead skuas. The two sole inhabitants of Nunatak Z had paid with their lives for our craving for fresh meat. I couldn't help reflecting that that pair of skuas had real cause to complain of their misfortune. In the aeons of time since this planet first took its shape no man had ever visited this desolate spot. No man may ever visit it again. Those two poor unfortunates had chosen the one hour of the one day when such a visit was to prove immediately fatal.

Later we discovered a Weddel seal and pup in a sheltered corner near the nunatak. This was a sizeable quantity of food for the dogs. How real their needs were, was demonstrated when with a rifle on the sledge I descended with the team to kill them. My normally well-behaved dogs fell on the two seals like famished wolves, before I had a chance to unsling the rifle, tearing at the sides of the living animals. With difficulty I succeeded in beating them back with the butt of the carbine, for the taste of warm blood made them quite insensitive to the lash of the whip.

Two shots and the writhing seals were put out of their agony. While skinning the seals, I suffered several assaults from the dogs. Even the normally indifferent Fram joined in the attempt of the rest of the team to reach the reeking meat. It was not until their hunger was assuaged a little with strips of still warm blubber that I was able to continue the butchering uninterrupted. The dogs that had been left behind at the weasels went mad with excitement when they saw the sledge-load of steaming seal meat approaching.

Rivolier saw the pathetic carcass of the baby seal lashed across the sledge.

'Murderer. Assassin of babies!' he accused.

However, he too agreed that the assassination was justified when he tasted the tender meat of the baby seal. The meat of a full-grown seal is black and tough, and though we were well accustomed to it, frequently asserting that it was indistinguishable from a good steak, there was never any doubt that we were eating seal. Not that seal meat is unpleasant, there is no oily taste, but it does have a distinctive flavour. However, this meat of the month-old seal pup was a bright, healthy red. It was so tender it seemed to melt in the mouth and was indistinguishable from a selected fillet of beef.

Outside, the dogs lay in dreamy ecstasy; in front of each were a few uneaten scraps. As I had promised, each dog had eaten his fill that night. Tomorrow it would be back to rations but who cared for tomorrow? Certainly not the dogs, for the present was perfection.

Rivolier celebrated the successful arrival with a superlative effort of cuisine. From the death of the two skuas and a tin of concentrated wine he gave us *Coq au Vin*, cooked in the style of Terre Adélie.

That night a blizzard drew an impenetrable veil over the satisfied participants, canine and human, of this gastronomic orgy. The blizzard raged the whole of the next day, and it was two days before Rivolier and I left with a dog team to visit Rocher X. There we camped to carry out observations on its position and on the periodicity of the tides, leaving Vincent and Marret at the weasel camp. We made a pleasant camp on the land-based ice at the shore of the island, and began work.

There were six pairs of skuas nesting on the island and in some of the nests we found fresh eggs. But this was all the life there was at Rocher X. The most annoying duty was the tidal observations. This entailed reading at half-hourly intervals a theodolite strapped to a bamboo stake driven in the floating sea ice. The readings had to be uninterrupted over twenty-four hours, or the whole series had to be recommenced. We prayed for twenty-four hours of fine weather, then set to work dividing the work into four shifts of which we each did two. The half-hourly interval was particularly annoying. It just gave time to put on boots, emerge from the shelter of the tent, adjust the theodolite, make the necessary readings, return to the tent, take off boots, and begin to relax. Then it would be time to go out for the next reading. Rivolier was not too familiar with this sort of work. Fearing that if he made an error during his tour we would have to start a fresh series, I warned him:

'If anything goes wrong, don't hesitate to wake me up.'

Rivolier gave an ugly leer. 'Don't worry, I will not hesitate a second!' Then, when finally the series was safely completed, he remarked, 'Of all the idiotic ways of spending an uncomfortable twenty-four hours, this takes not only the cake but the icing as well.'

We were just on the verge of packing up for return to the weasels, when we heard a 'halloo' and found that Vincent and Marret with the second dog team were with us. They had left Bjorn and his team on the sea ice below us to avoid a fight between teams.

It was on this day that the battle for supremacy between Fram and Bjorn took place. For months now we had been expecting it, then it came as a complete surprise when the two dogs decided the question of kingship on the sea ice below us. More annoying still was that we could only deduce what happened. Fram as was customary was roaming free, but what we did not know was that Astro, his big white lieutenant, was also loose. While we were chatting in the tent, Fram and Astro prowling along the tide crack, found themselves ten feet above the sleeping and unprepared Bjorn. The first intimation Bjorn had of battle was when about two hundred pounds of dog in two snarling lumps dropped out of the heavens upon him.

Fram had, in his wisdom, waited a long while for this opportunity. He had more than countered Bjorn's strength and battle experience by intelligence, but even so neither he or Astro, who fought for Fram, had an easy victory. They were both mauled and scarred when they returned, leaving a beaten Bjorn on the sea ice behind them. We could only imagine what this epic battle had been like, so serious that it had been fought silently.

We pictured Bjorn suddenly awakened to find the most decisive battle in his life already in progress, not against one dog but against two; two dogs that through past training moved as though directed by one mind; with Fram slashing at his throat and head while Astro worried his flanks. Perhaps if the battle had been joined after preliminary skirmishes, he might yet have won for he was an enormously powerful dog and seemed almost impervious to punishment. But the battle was half-lost to him before he knew it had commenced. He probably tried to concentrate on Astro, trying with a swift attack to put the lesser enemy out of action before turning his attention to the principal attacker. But Fram must have been too cunning for that, pressing the attack until Bjorn lay exhausted and whimpering on the ground while his vanquishers slashed at him with cruel and punishing bites, each one calculated to drive home into Bjorn's pain-tormented mind that both of these dogs could beat him, not only in this battle but in any future one.

So at Rocher X, two hundred miles from home, Fram won the kingship of all the dogs.

A little later when we had all returned to the weasel's camp and were sitting around a mug of coffee Marret remarked:

'As the first people to visit Rocher X we now have the right to give it a name. Any suggestions?'

Vincent, the irrepressible, exclaimed with an air of earnestness!

'I have exactly the name!'

'What?'

'Let's call it Rocher Y!'

9

Finale

What is leadership?

Some men assume its mantle easily, on others it sits, not only uncomfortably, but also ungracefully. All claim its privileges on the least pretext, but only those who are born to lead shoulder its responsibilities squarely. Marret never demonstrated his right to the leadership of his party more than in his decision at Nunatak Z to stay with the weasels, while we, the other three, under Rivolier, went on with the dogs westward over the sea ice along the coast.

The seasonal break-out of the sea ice was close, and there is always a certain amount of risk attached to any sledging journey. If anything happened to the party, Marret, on his return, would face criticism of the worst kind for not accompanying his men forward. For us in the field his decision needed no justification, but for those in Paris who might judge him, such a course of action could be construed in a bad light. Marret accepted this risk, a much more worrying one than driving his weasel over a crevasse bridge, which he had done so many times. He accepted it because it was the best for the group. Someone had to stay with the weasels for a number of reasons; firstly to maintain a radio link between the dog teams and the base, secondly, to keep the weasels in running order, and lastly to be capable of driving one weasel back, alone, to a pre-selected rendezvous on the plateau behind Glacier Z, in case of the sea ice breaking out and the dog teams being forced to return by the plateau in a long sweep south of Glacier Z. After weighing up the requirements, and assessing the capabilities of the four men available, Marret decided that he, himself, was the best equipped to carry out this task. So, sacrificing his own very natural desire to go on with the dogs on the last leg of the journey, he elected to stay on alone, while Rivolier led the dog teams. This was leadership at its best. It is easy to go forward, it takes a big man to stay behind.

The dogs were made up into two teams. The leading team was Fram's but now reduced to Fram, Helen, Astro, Seismo, Roald, and Pomme, while Wild and Maru of this team joined Bjorn's team which now consisted of these two, Bjorn, Milk and Tiki. Fram's team, being the stronger, led. It was more capable of breaking a fresh trail, thus easing the problem of driving the second team, which with a sledge track to follow requires little direction. Having Fram as the leader of the first sledge in the difficult conditions encountered was the major element in keeping the sledges moving forward. He proved to be at his very best in the broken terrain that we encountered.

Because of the imminence of a break-out, it was decided to travel as close to the coastal ice cliff as possible. To do this meant cutting across Glacier Z and other glaciers to the west close to the land, where the icebergs making up the glacier tongues lie closely packed in a continuous barrier. This meant we had to force a passage through the great walls of floating ice frozen between the bergs. We did not realize at the beginning what we had undertaken in trying to travel through the tongue of Glacier Z.

The utter chaos of distorted ice and broken bergs beggared description. To begin with, the bergs were almost cemented together, though here and there narrow lanes existed, twisting among towering walls of sapphire blue ice. But the sea ice between these walls was so distorted by the pressure of the million-ton monsters as to be well-nigh impassable. Forcing a passage meant following these tortuous passages into the heart of the glacier tongue. It was like wandering in a hopeless maze, a maze covering six hundred square miles and built by mischievous giants.

We encountered the east wall of the tongue of Glacier Z soon after leaving the weasel camp, and travelled northward along the side of it, probing here and there into any re-entrant that offered hope of a passage. The first passage began as a wide amphitheatre which promised well, but, after we had travelled several miles into it, the walls began to close down rapidly, until we found ourselves halted by a continuous barrier of ice standing one hundred and fifty feet sheer above the level of the frozen sea. There was nothing to be done but to turn back and try again.

The next passage was not as promising, but as we pushed forward, although frequently the ice wall ahead seemed unbroken, on arrival at what seemed an impassable barrier we would find a narrow cleft, hidden by irregularities of the icebergs, where the dogs and sledges could squeeze through and continue.

Apart from this bewildering chaos of tumbled ice and massive bergs, the surface itself was unbelievably bad. We soon forgot what a normal snowfield looked like; the plateau with its sastrugi was a billiard table compared with this confusion of tilted and rafted ice floes. Imagine a section of ocean filled with pieces of ice scattered broadcast, ranging in size from leviathans ten miles by ten miles down to fragments the size of a tennis ball, all frozen together at haphazard angles, except for open leads of water still persisting here and there. Carpet this confusion with a ten-foot thick layer of soft snow and you have some idea of what conditions existed in the tongue of the glacier. The carpet of snow did not help at all; it only served to mask the leads and crevasses, so that both men and dogs found themselves breaking through the snow into hidden water.

We had to follow the gaps that existed among the bergs; we could not choose our direction, for that was already decided for us. Landmarks did not exist; in that profusion of fantastic ice shapes each piece was so complex in form that they all appeared the same. The drifting snow buried our sledge tracks as we passed. Only the sun showing weakly through the altostratus cloud told us that we were making progress, for without it, we could be heading towards any point of the compass.

The sledges began to break up under the terrific punishment that they were taking. The dogs lost all spring to their movements, and with their heads down pulled doggedly ahead.

Fram was always in the lead. He was continually looking back at the sledge, so that when the equipment lurched on a dangerous ice slope, without a word from his driver, he would bring his team to one side to save the sledge slipping sideways to disaster. When running along narrow snow cornices, with a drop of a hundred feet on either side, there was no need to shout directions to Fram; before the driver could decide what should be done, Fram would have taken the necessary action and averted the danger. On the rare occasions that I found myself with an upturned sledge lying in a crevice in the ice, I could not blame Fram, for Fram had merely obeyed my orders against his better judgment. More and more on that trip, I realized that the fewer orders that I gave to Fram the less trouble we had. It seemed to me at times that Fram was an extension of my own brain, that all I had to do was think, and Fram would execute my thoughts.

The following sledge, with Bjorn's team, were not finding it so easy. They were a weak team at best, and now this weakness was painfully apparent. Bjorn, following his defeat by Fram, was completely demoralized. He made no attempt to lead, in fact, he was barely pulling his weight as a team member. The old Bjorn had been a great dog in harness, not intelligent, but very much the leader. He had always annoyed us by his bumptious bullying of his team, but now all was changed; anarchy was rife, and Bjorn was behaving like a terror-stricken coward. Tiki, normally the most timid of dogs, who never before had fought a battle, being always protected by his friend Milk, became quarrelsome, and seemed, incredibly enough, to be actually making a bid for leadership. Maru, the penguin-killer, was the least affected. He was not by nature aggressive, so, since he was easy-going and controllable, on him fell the virtual leadership. Wild was too young, while Tiki's friend Milk was too puzzled by the sudden change in the effeminate Tiki to be able to concentrate on orders. I did not envy Rivolier and Vincent the task of keeping their sledge moving with this disorganized team.

During the whole journey we never escaped from this maze of coastal icebergs and glacier. It was impossible to tell whether we had crossed the tongue of Glacier Z and were encountering fresh glaciers, or whether the whole tangled mass of ice could be grouped as being one continuous glacier. The crowning blow was a week of overcast skies during which we never saw the sun. We could see nothing; sky, cloud, icebergs, obstacles and surface all blended into one indistinguishable whiteness. Frequently the sledge would be pulled up suddenly against a sheer wall of ice that was invisible in this light, or else dogs, driver and sledge would go hurtling over an ice cliff that was not seen at all. With no idea of direction and no observations of position, progress became slower and slower. Everything was the same flat whiteness about us. Trying to find a route ahead was pure Blind Man's Buff. We might as well have been blind for all the use our eyes were to us in picking a route.

Pomme distinguished himself at one overnight camp by eating a fifteen-foot sealskin whip. I came out of the tent in the morning to find him at the final stage of this repast. He had managed most of his fifteen-foot meal, and he stood there with a dreamy expression in his eyes, masticating gently, with the butt of the whip still hanging sadly out of his mouth. Travelling that day the meal upset him and he vomited lengths of the whip at intervals. These were snapped up by the other dogs immediately.

Rivolier added to my enjoyment of the journey by upsetting a cooker full of pemmican into the open mouth of my sleeping-bag. Vincent promptly moved that, since I had received three men's rations there, I would not be entitled to any more food for the next three meals and could lie in my sleeping-bag and suck the fabric!

Fram and Astro were free one night. A terrified scream from Bjorn, a brief scuffle, then the sound of Bjorn whimpering like a hurt puppy, told us that Astro had broken loose and had joined Fram, who was as usual free. Bjorn was hopeless the next day; not only hopeless in harness, but so demoralized as to give continual trouble running loose. He followed at a distance of several hundred yards to be sure of being clear of further attacks by Fram and Astro. He was so terrified now that when a man tried to pat him, he screamed with unreasoning fear. At times we would look back and find that Bjorn was no longer following. A search back along the sledge tracks would reveal him, curled up in the shelter of a pinnacle of ice, whimpering to himself, wishing nothing more than to be left alone to die. Sometimes, to keep him with us, we had to drag him on a trailing rope from the rear of the sledge.

The next day we were blizzard-bound in the tent. All night we heard the cry of a seal very close to the tent. Towards midday I went out with the carbine in the blizzard to look for it. I loosed Astro and Fram, taking them with me, trusting them to lead me to it, for in the driving snow I could see nothing, not even the dark bulk of a seal. Astro was delighted, and stayed with me the whole time, but Fram could not bring himself to leave his team and Helen. After a short distance he stopped, hesitated a minute then bounded back to his team. After an hour's futile searching in the blizzard, I gave up the hunt, and found my way back by following Astro to the tent. Fram joined him near the tent, and before I could stop them the two of them dived on a curled-up mass in the snow. Poor Bjorn was being attacked again.

We only made four miles the next day. Instead of passing through the glacier tongue to better travelling, the farther we penetrated the worse it became. The sledges were patched wrecks from the steady pounding they had received. We halted at three o'clock that afternoon, not because we were tired, which we were, but because we could advance no further. The way ahead seemed barred. A reconnaissance ahead on skis confirmed this. A man travelling light on skis can cover most terrain rapidly, but here skis were little aid to progress, so we had no chance of getting the dogs farther. This was to be our outer limit. The skies were still overcast, so we were obliged to camp in order to await the appearance of the sun to fix the position of our last outward camp.

Pomme got highly excited when a seal blew in a narrow crevice beneath where he was tied. The big, clumsy dog, catching the scent of the seal through the snow, began to dig madly to get at it. As the sea ice here was old, and about forty feet thick, we thought it unlikely that success would crown his efforts, but Pomme had a one-track mind, so for the whole period he dug steadily.

Within the tent, Rivolier and I growled at Vincent. Accustomed as we two were to sharing the tent between the two of us, we begrudged Vincent the room he was taking up. We told him that in common decency he should sleep out on the snow flaps outside. Vincent claimed that for all the room we two left him he might just as well do that.

That night, as we were tuning in our miniature radio receiver trying to get a time signal, by a freak of radio conditions we picked up a short-wave station, and heard a voice in French mention 'La Terre Adélie.' The station was Radio Saigon and the voice proved to be that of Yves Vallette, explaining to his radio audience that he was passing through Saigon on his way to Australia where he would join the ship *Tottan* to go down with it to the Antarctic to supervise our relief. At this very moment, he said, a small party were away on an important journey and were camped near the 137th meridian of east longitude. Rivolier snorted with disgust, and contradicted the receiver.

'Not the 137th meridian, the 136th. Our progress hasn't been that bad.'

There was considerable doubt, however, as to precisely where we were. Our position was finally calculated as being 136 degrees 9 minutes, or less than three miles from the border of French and Australian territories, so our jaunt forward on skis must have taken us very close indeed to the 136th meridian, which was the accepted border with Wilkes Land.

We broke camp and began the return to the weasels. We managed to sight here and there a faint mark on the ridges of snow that told us we were following our outward track. This was a great help, and with our diminished loads, speeded up our return. The second team now had a partially recovered Bjorn back in harness and although he still was not leading, his great strength made it possible to keep up with the leading team.

Fram's sense of humour annoyed me. In the twisted ice of the glacier tongue he was irreproachable, but when we broke out of the maze onto a good travelling surface, he seemed to decide that he had done his part. I called 'Yuck' and Fram turned obediently, too obediently, to the left, and continued to turn until he had made a half-circle. I called 'Heely' and he turned as much right as he had turned left. So it continued, until our sledge tracks behind resembled the marks of a skater making figures-of-eight. The more I screamed with rage, the more exasperating Fram became. Finally, infuriated and smarting under jibes from Vincent, I halted the sledge, drove in a mooring-pin, uncoiled the whip from the sledge handle-bars and walked forward to Fram. The other dogs scattered to each side. Thereafter the sledge track ran as though ruled with a straight-edge across the plain of snow.

We came in on the weasel camp from the north. Although it was ten o'clock at night, and an unpleasant wind with medium drift was blowing off the plateau, the moment the weasels hove in sight we saw Marret waving a welcome from the weasel roof. He was very glad indeed to see us, having found his lonely vigil at the weasel camp more trying than he had anticipated. He had set fire to a weasel on one occasion, and poisoned himself with a tin of preserved food on another. Being alone, he was unable to venture far from the vehicles because of the danger of crevasses, so the only bright spot each day had been his nightly radio contact with Lépineux at the base.

Before leaving Nunatak Z, we built a cairn of rock on the highest point of land, in which we placed a sealed can with a note to the next visitor, if there ever would be one, wrapped around a flask containing three nips of rum. A rapid dog sledge trip eastward along the coast had completed the work in the area, and when the weasel motors turned over again we were on the return journey, with our backs turned to Glacier Z.

On the last few days before arrival at Nunatak Z we had let Milk and Tiki run free alongside the weasels. They had behaved very well, always running a few hundred yards ahead of the weasels. We decided to adopt the same procedure on our return, harnessing the other dogs except for Bjorn, into Fram's team, and letting Milk and Tiki run free. We had only made a few miles when we found that they were no longer with us. I went back with the dog team to find them. They were nowhere to be seen, but on the lee side of the nunatak I found them. Apparently they had decided to stay behind and set up house for themselves, for they had dug out a hole in the snow alongside a rock, and were curled up together there, perfectly happy. The only way I could bring them on was to tie them both on the trailing rope of my sledge and drag them bodily until we caught up with the weasels. Once back at the weasels, now out of sight of the sea, they gave no further trouble, running ahead of the weasels as they had done before.

The return was almost without event. Snow conditions had improved since the outward journey and our daily averages were excellent. The last day into Camp Six was the best of all. We made a hundred and two miles in thirty-two hours, with the weasels running non-stop to take advantage of an excellent surface. This was fine for the machines that know no fatigue, but, after the first thirty miles, the dogs began to drop farther and farther behind. The only way to keep going was to carry the dogs on the weasel sledges. When we tied them on the sledges they were suspicious and nervous, but after an hour or so of travelling without the least effort on their part, they were all sitting up looking most satisfied with life.

'Hmmm,' I growled to Marret, whose idea it had been. 'After a day or two of this, they will never pull a sledge again. It's only because they know nothing else better that they can be persuaded to pull.'

A tragedy however was impending. Tiki began to act strangely, biting at everything in reach in the weasel barge, from a crowbar to a tent, and even his bosom friend Milk.

We were hurrying as hard as we dared push the weasels, in order to be back before the ice in the bay between Géologie and Ile des Pétrels broke out, for we needed that ice as a road. Because of limited accommodation for the dogs in the sledges and barges, we had to rest the dogs in shifts; half were carried in the sledges, while the other half ran free alongside the weasels. At forty miles from Camp Six it became Milk and Tiki's turn to run free. Since they had had plenty of experience at following the weasels, we let the pair of them loose without any worries. Ten miles farther on, we were horrified to find no sign of them. We halted several hours, hoping that they would catch up, but we saw no sign of the two. However as they had the clear marks of the weasel tracks to follow we decided to push on to Camp Six. That was the last we ever saw of Milk and Tiki. Perhaps they acted as they did at Nunatak Z and dug a hole into the sastrugi and curled up in it, or else stumbled and went hurtling into a crevasse. We were inclined to blame Tiki for the loss, and felt it was a miserable finish for the gallant Milk, who, despite the fearful wounds he had received early on the journey, had pulled his sledge courageously.

Even at Camp Six, the following day, we expected them to come roaming in, for they were used to following the weasel tracks, and the tracks were showing very clearly. To help them, we left them ample supplies of seal meat, so that for the last twenty-five miles from Camp Six to the base they would not be hungry.

After a day's halt at Camp Six, waiting for them and setting up the Camp Six Depot with our surplus stores, we started the last twenty-five miles back to Ile des Pétrels. The crevasses, where Vincent had nearly lost his weasel, were now showing up very clearly. A long smooth band, like a wide road across the sastrugi, showed the position of each snow bridge. Marret, as usual driving the leading weasel, did not even bother to dismount to examine them before crossing. He just drove alongside each one for a short distance, then drove across, after first telling his passenger to jump out, so in case the bridge did not bear the weasel, there would be only one man, himself, lost.

The last obstacle was the steep descent over bare blue ice to Pointe Géologie. Going up had been easy, for there had been more snow covering the ice, and the weasels had been pulling their sledges behind them upwards. But going down the sledges kept getting out of control, overrunning the weasels. The slope was finally negotiated by forming a train, with the rearward weasel acting as a brake and all the sledges roped between it and the leading weasel.

Four hours later the weasels were back at base, and the journey and, for that matter, the year's work were over. All that remained for us was to fill in the few weeks until the arrival of the *Tottan*. Between the two weasels that had returned, there were only four main springs unbroken instead of the eight they should have had. It had not only been the dogs that felt the strain of the race home.

The two missing dogs, Milk and Tiki, were expected to return daily; each morning as soon as we woke we would look to the dog lines, hoping to see them back in their places with their team. Poor creatures, without a man to care for them they could not hope to last long. Perhaps they saw the sea in the distance and tried to descend to the coast, perhaps one fell through a snowbridge into a crevasse and the survivor, mourning his friend, remained peering into the dark abyss, whimpering and lost, until cold and hunger claimed him too.

Another casualty, while we were away, had been Nelson, who had gone into a rapid decline shortly after we left. Georges had tried to care for him, but he did not respond to treatment and gradually became weaker and weaker. His mind, never very stable, deteriorated with his body. Then towards the end he began to suffer severe pain. Georges put the .45 pistol into his pocket and took Nelson for a short walk. Nelson, who had always feared men, ceased to fear or feel anything any more.

Aspirin, still chained to the rubbish barge, dozed away his days, lying in a cesspit of filth.

A touching scene was the reunion of Bjorn and Ifaut, separated by the journey. It was like husband and wife coming together after a long absence. Bjorn showed her his half-healed wounds, and she licked them with feminine sympathy, baring her teeth at Fram who was chained nearby. After a few days near Ifaut, Bjorn had recovered most of his old spirit.

But over the dog lines was the shadow of death. Paris had not been able to discover a new home for them once we closed down the station and returned. The only course that lay open to us was to shoot them, for they would be condemned to a lingering death if they were left alone here.

It was sad to walk the dog lines, past each of our canine comrades, each of whom followed our progress with trusting and friendly eyes, and to think that soon the man whom they regarded as their friend and protector was to be their executioner. It was now a long time since they had seemed a motley and indistinguishable mob. Now each one was a very definite personality with its character known to us as well as our own. It was interesting to note that each man volunteered to carry out the execution of his own favourite dog. Each wanted to be sure that the dog would be put away without knowing what was happening. The thought of taking old Boss on his last walk was a sad one. As for Fram . . .

Then one day Marret called me into the radio room.

'Our dogs are saved!' he said, showing me a telegram from Paul-Émile Victor, the leader of *Expeditions Polaires Françaises,* saying that satisfactory arrangements had now been made for the return of the dogs to France, even the old useless veterans like Boss and Aspirin. We had never even dared to hope that Boss and Aspirin would be reprieved, even if the young dogs were. Thus, the arrival of the ship was now to be a signal for complete rejoicing.

Christmas day was celebrated as well as our vanishing food supplies would permit. As the ship was on its way to us, the pantry could be raided freely. Georges Lépineux, who had guarded his precious groceries against our depredations throughout the year, relaxed his vigilance. More than that, he produced a packing-case crammed with luxuries that he had hidden many months ago, unknown to any of us. It was a most magnificent repast.

Seven days later the tall crow's nest of the *Tottan* was seen over the horizon. The motorboat seemed an interminably long time being lowered and in covering the few miles to shore. After a long year that seemed to have passed away almost unnoticed, this last hour seemed interminable.

No one slept that night. The hut table was piled with letters, parcels and periodicals. There was so much that had gone on in the outside world that we knew little about. First, of course, were the letters. Each was read that night, for, though radio telegrams had kept us in touch, there was so much in the letters that no telegram could cover. I saw photographs of my daughter Janet, born shortly after my departure the year before. One by one my wife's letters introduced me to this new member of our family. I sat very silently on the end of my bunk reading far into the night.

The next day the work of packing up the station began. Since there was no relief party the station had to be closed down temporarily for several years. This meant the return of most of the valuable gear to France and the shutting up of the hut for the last time.

Marret had a last trip to make. With the ship was Pierre Stahl, a gravimetrist who wished to take a line of measurements on the plateau behind Port Martin. It was necessary also for me to take some observations at Cap Pépin on the coast to the west. Accordingly, Prévost was left alone at the hut at Ile des Pétrels, while the rest of the party embarked on the *Tottan* and sailed for Port Martin. Here one weasel was disembarked at the burnt-out station for Marret, Stahl and Vallette to make a quick trip south on the plateau. A further group also disembarked at Port Martin to salvage any valuable stores that had been spared by the fire. The *Tottan*, with Rivolier and I aboard, then sailed for Cap Pépin. We were standing off Cap Pépin in thick weather when we received a signal by radio from Port Martin announcing that Duhamel had met with an accident. One finger had been badly crushed and Rivolier, our surgeon, was needed back immediately. So the ship hurried back to Port Martin. As soon as Duhamel came aboard, Rivolier, aided by Lépineux, operated and by doing so saved the finger.

It had been a freak accident. It was ironic after such an eventful year that our only casualty was to occur when the tour of duty was virtually over. Duhamel had been carrying a heavy sledge-hammer over one shoulder when he slipped on the ice. Automatically he put one hand out to stop his fall and, as he did so, the heavy hammer slipped off his shoulder and struck his outstretched hand, crushing it against the hard ice. Even if one tried deliberately, it would be difficult to duplicate such an accident.

Marret's plans for this last phase had been complex; three men in a weasel on the plateau, four men on shore at Port Martin, one man alone at Ile des Pétrels, and two men cruising with the ship. Now, with the accident to Duhamel, he had to simplify the position. Accordingly, we re-embarked all the Port Martin group and called in at Ile des Pétrels to pick up Prévost and the dogs, on our way back to Port Martin. Meanwhile Marret, Stahl and Vallette left for the south in the weasel.

As we went ashore at Ile des Pétrels to pick up Prévost, we found the last little pieces of sheltered bay ice broken loose and bumping about in the bay. The last of the Emperor Penguins sat nervously on these pieces to drift away northward into the southern ocean. Adelie penguins were everywhere, sporting in the water or standing in fussy groups about the shore. The loose floes, jostling one another in the bay, made it difficult to load dogs and stores. It was impossible to hold the boat at one point for any length of time, for the heavy floes would close in on it to threaten it with disaster.

It was almost with nostalgia that we visited the hut that had been our home so long for the last time. But its tidiness, Prévost having arranged everything ready to leave, struck an alien note. The hut we were going to remember was an untidy, crowded place full of personality, while this was just a clean room. Without regret, we closed the door for the last time and secured it with nails, then trooped down to the waiting boat. Fram's team, which had been working to the very last, were driven to the edge of the water. Their traces were cut and one by one they were lowered, still in their harness, into the waiting boat.

After carrying out the work at Cap Pépin, the ship returned to Port Martin to re-embark the weasel party who, their mission successfully completed, were awaiting us. Here, I was fortunate in having an hour or so ashore to wander over the burnt-out station. The last time I had seen it was in mid-winter under the light of the moon, as we strove to start our weasels and escape from it with the stores we had salvaged. Now in mid-summer with the sun shining brightly it seemed a more pleasant place. It was hard to believe that here we had had such a desperate struggle, with the success of the venture swinging on a hair. Only the sight of a packing-case broken open on the rocks, exactly as I had left it six months ago, convinced me that all this had really happened.

We sailed for Australia that night. I stood on the after-deck looking back, and, in the distance I could see the bright light of the midnight sun showing reddish on the plateau. A little later that too was gone, and at all points of the compass our horizon was the boundless sea. Astern the white wake bubbled, and the ship nosed deep into the heaving swell. This was goodbye to Adélie Land and a year of adventure and endeavour. As I walked below I heard the dogs whimpering nervously in their new environment. Soon even the link that they provided would be gone too.

The men are now home, I in Australia, and my six comrades in France. The dogs went back to France too. Fram's team is pulling a sledge at Chamonix, while the others are scattered, mainly among the mountains of France. Two, I think, deserve special mention. Aspirin has found a new and congenial home; he lives with a pastry-cook. Knowing Aspirin, I am sure he will make full use of the capabilities of his new master. Boss is the other—Boss, who had known the full gamut of a husky's life, had been born among the Eskimos in Greenland, served as team member, fought his way to leadership, and finally had been deposed after years of service. This old veteran, who, in the normal way of things, would have been eased to a well-earned rest with a bullet in his skull, found a closing chapter to his years so just that I hesitate to record it, for fear of being accused of romancing.

If you should watch from the wall surrounding a certain gracious home not far from Paris, you would see, in the morning, a servant arrive with a bowl of chocolate in front of a spacious kennel. A grizzled, scarred old dog would emerge to receive it. He then would be taken into the centre of the garden, to a tree that now by right is his, where he would lie most of the day, warming his old bones under a friendly northern sun, interrupted only when at midday they would bring his bowl of soup, and he, now accustomed to such attentions, does not even get on to his feet to accept it, but leans his head over the bowl, and laps it up still lying on his side. So Boss is now lazing out his last years in the sunshine, visited frequently by his human friends, and idolized by the lady who volunteered to provide a home for him. No one who knew the grand old dog would dispute his claim to this.

As the reader has seen, sledge dogs, or huskies, are complex characters. The stern life that they lead hardens them, physically and mentally, to fit them for what their masters want of them, which is not friendship, but unflinching and unrewarded service up to the point of death. They are just mongrels of no known ancestry, but the strain of the wolf is strong in them. The human hand that stretches out to pat the head of the dog recoils as the lips draw back to show the fangs of the wolf. The team becomes identified with the pack, with leadership the prize of battle. Anything weak and helpless falls victim to their destructive fangs, and around the camp one hears, not the friendly bark of dogs, but the mournful howl of the wolf. In battle, they are cruel and vicious, dealing out horrible wounds among themselves. But their driver, and for that matter, any man, can walk into a seething mass of twenty battle-crazed dogs, cuffing the snapping, snarling beasts across their snouts with his bare hands with complete impunity; to them the man is sacred. He, the man, occupies a rank above the leader, and the symbol of his power is the whip. And symbol it is, for it is not the sting of its lash, but its implied threat that makes the whip bulk large in the eyes of the dogs. The worst dogs are those that have been driven by cuts of the whip, for they become used to its sting, which, in reality, is hardly felt when compared with the wounds they give each other in battle. So, the whip, too well known to them, loses its authority. With a well-trained team, it is possible to drive by word of command, leaving the whip where it should be, coiled over the handlebars of the sledge, only to be used on rare occasions, when its crack to one side of the team will bring them swiftly round to avoid a danger. Other than that, a call to the leader, holding the coiled whip high in one hand for him to see, is sufficient reminder to him that he must obey more promptly. Dogs, like humans, fear the imaginary much more than the real.

The relationship between man and husky is not that of man and pet; it is a working partnership. In rare cases one finds a leader like Fram who, by reason of intelligence superior to that of the normal dog, becomes more of a partner than a subordinate. Such dogs are rare, perhaps one in a hundred, but once found they are beyond value. Fram was never a pet, not because I did not try to make one of him, but because he refused to debase his natural dignity for the cheap caresses of a man.

It was a sad few minutes for me when I took leave of Fram at the ship's side in Australia. It was like saying farewell for the last time to a very old and dear friend. We had seen the good and the bad of sledge travel together; seen the breathless stillness and beauty of the polar plateau, when the skies are clear and the light and colour painful in its sapphire purity, and we had marched together into driving drift with the ice forming masks about our faces. Now it was ended. I was back with my wife and daughter in Australia, and Fram was sailing for France. How could anyone understand Fram, who did not know him as I did, who did not know how magnificent he could be when the snow was soft and deep so the sledge sank to its bridges amid a terrain torn and riven into a chaos of broken ice, or who did not know how exasperating he could be when the going was so easy as to be unworthy of his talents. A last pat, and Fram went out of my life, leaving a gap that no other dog could fill.

Occasionally I am asked to give a lecture on experiences in the Antarctic. I tell this story, or others very like it, and invariably, at the end of the ordeal (for I am a poor speaker), there are questions, and equally invariably, one of these questions is one that, perhaps, the reader is asking now.

'I found all this interesting, but why do men go on expeditions to such a barren, worthless and inhospitable land?'

It is a legitimate question, but difficult to answer.

The economic possibilities of Antarctica are hard to assess. There is little hope of immediate gain, for the great landmass of Antarctica, mantled by a 2,000-foot-thick sheet of permanent ice, guards its treasures jealously and is loth to yield its secrets. Antarctica is a cold, indifferent and most times cruel mistress towards her lovers. She gives little and demands much both in effort and endurance.

Geologically, it appears that Antarctica is generally similar to South America and South Africa, its mineral possibilities being by deduction the same as those countries. But the prospecting of Antarctica presents a problem similar to prospecting a land in which only the tops of the highest mountains are visible, with all the lowlands denied to the seeker. The only clue he has to what lies beneath the ice sheet is given by the action of the ice itself, which, grinding slowly over the underlying rocks, tears them loose so that in time these free rocks from beneath the ice work to the surface and are found deposited on the glacial moraines.

Of land life there is none. Once the traveller leaves the coast for inland ice, he leaves all life behind him, for all the life is concentrated at the shore in the form of seals, penguins and sea birds that come from the sea. All of these save one, the Emperor penguin, leave when the darkness of winter sets in. A few primitive mosses and rudimentary lichens are found in sheltered corners, but otherwise there is no vegetation. Little is known of the fishes of the Antarctic coast. Members of the *notathenia* family, a bottom-loving rock cod, are caught all along the coastline but no other fishes are known to exist in quantity. The only immediately exploitable resources are the whale fisheries, which draw each season the great factory ships and their attendant whale chasers from Norway, England and Japan.

But for a world with a rapidly increasing population, the Antarctic waters have one great interest. For here in the cold, icy south lie great untapped reservoirs of food waiting to be harvested. This is plankton, the food of the whales and the penguins, minute plant and animal life that drifts with the ocean currents around the icy land in astronomical quantities. No other sea is as rich as the Antarctic sea in this respect.

So there is little chance of exploiting, in the immediate future, the wealth of Antarctica. Say, rather, that the first problem is to assess what exists in or about the great southern land. At this stage it is pure exploration, to look, to find, and to record.

It is certainly not hope of immediate financial gain that sends men willingly to live among the ice and blizzards. If commercial success had been the driving force behind the great explorations of other continents, many of those voyages would never have been carried out. For to the explorer the real goal is to further man's knowledge of this planet and the forces that govern it. He uses the promise of commercial possibilities, only half-believing in them, to gain backing for his enterprise. His ultimate aim is to seek, to find and, in doing so, to understand.

In a way it is also a sort of escapism. There seems to have been a marked deterioration of moral standards at all levels ranging from international behaviour to that of mere ordinary individuals. So much so, that modern living has reached a stage at which it demands a great degree of cynicism and selfishness to make it at all liveable, or else a standard of righteous indignation bordering on the fanatical. Much as we hesitate to admit it, the individual is being gradually sacrificed to the State even among the democracies. The idea of the individual man as a possessor of rights and liberties is being submerged in a spate of 'isms.' This is most convenient for the governing bodies of nations, for conduct which would be indefensible to an individual conscience can be justified by the needs of the shadowy ill-defined State. Much too often does one hear nowadays, 'Of course it is wrong, but what can I, one man, do about it?'

One comes away from the near hopeless complexities of modern life, with its half-hearted battling against intangible evils, to a clean fight against worthy opponents, the elements of wind, cold and ice. It is a struggle worthy of the best in men and one that cannot do less than honour the dignity of man as an individual. Against the vastness of the polar continent one realizes the microscopic insignificance of man in relation to the elements about him, but at the same time appreciates the important part man can play in the scheme of things, completely disproportionate to his relative size. Here one can find a sense of values, truer, I dare to think, than those that obsess us in the walks of civilization.

If this is escapism, then a considerable part of the motivation behind the polar explorer must come under this heading.

Men explore the frozen wastes for a variety of personal reasons, some worthy, others not so much so. But in all their efforts there is one driving force, that being to push the frontiers of man's knowledge of the vast unknown of which he is part, just a little farther. It is a desire in man, as inherent as sleeping or eating. Were it not so, we would still be living on the uncooked flesh of beasts in caverns, little better in thought and action than the beasts themselves.

The vast unknown of the Antarctic continent is a challenge to the inquiring mind of man. I am glad that there are many who have taken up that challenge, men like Marret, Prévost, Vincent, Rivolier, Duhamel and Lépineux with whom I served, simple men who have found themselves worthy, and in doing so, have proved that all men, despite their individual misgivings, are equally worthy of doing battle with the forces of nature or for that matter even with the evils of modern civilization. It is an earnest that man as an individual is not dead; he merely sleeps a while, and when he awakens, is capable of remedying what is not right around him if he so desires.

The most comforting thought I have derived from this work, and incidentally too from the beastliness of war, is a realization of the boundless possibilities that lie within the most ordinary of men; that all men, given the right stimulus, are capable of the finest of deeds; that great deeds are not the prerogative of a selected few, but are within the potentialities of every man.

If for nothing else, such work is well worth while.